DATE DUE

DEC 1 9 1980			

JOSTEN'S 30 508

Clothing for the Handicapped, the Aged, and Other People with Special Needs

Clothing for the Handicapped, the Aged, and Other People with Special Needs

By

ADELINE M. HOFFMAN, Ph.D.

Professor Emeritus
Department of Home Economics
University of Iowa
Iowa City, Iowa

With a Foreword by

Woodrow W. Morris, Ph.D.

Associate Dean, College of Medicine
University of Iowa
Iowa City, Iowa

Illustrations by

Lonnie M. Kennedy

CHARLES C THOMAS • PUBLISHER
Springfield • Illinois • U.S.A.

Published and Distributed Throughout the World by

CHARLES C THOMAS • PUBLISHER

Bannerstone House

301-327 East Lawrence Avenue, Springfield, Illinois, U.S.A.

© *1979, by* CHARLES C THOMAS • PUBLISHER

ISBN 0-398-03860-0

Library of Congress Catalog Card Number: 78-12729

With THOMAS BOOKS *careful attention is given to all details of
manufacturing and design. It is the Publisher's desire to present books that
are satisfactory as to their physical qualities and artistic possibilities and
appropriate for their particular use.* THOMAS BOOKS *will be true to those
laws of quality that assure a good name and good will.*

Printed in the United States of America
· *V-R-1*

Library of Congress Cataloging in Publication Data

Hoffman, Adeline Mildred.
    Clothing for the handicapped, the aged, and other
people with special needs.

    Includes index.
    1. Handicapped--Clothing.   2. Aged--Clothing.
I. Title.
TT648.H63   391   78-12729
ISBN 0-398-03860-0

To Mary Eleanor Brown, Eleanor Boettke Hotte, Murial E. Zimmerman and the late Helen Cookman, Van Davis Odell, and Iva M. Bader, for their recent contributions to the field of clothing for people with special needs; to Mary Catherine Beasley, Kay Caddel, Mary Murphy, and Linda Thiel, for their current contributions; to all those who have contributed to the total effort in creating clothing to satisfy the various specific needs encountered by many people, and who have helped to disseminate information through journal articles and other publications, and workshops, seminars and conferences, to reach those in need and those who will teach others.

FOREWORD

THIS book can be important to a variety of groups of people because it is designed to call attention to and to seek appropriate consideration for an important element of everyday living — the ways and means by which elderly and handicapped persons with special needs may clothe themselves.

This book can be important to home economists who make a specialty of considering the clothing needs of society since it directs them into paths which have often been overlooked.

This book can be important to clinicians of all types — those physicians who care for the elderly and handicapped; nurses who provide more intimate day-to-day care; occupational therapists who are concerned with the development of adaptive skills to cope with the tasks of daily living; physical therapists who are concerned with the prevention of disabilities, particularly of the musculoskeletal system; psychologists who need to be aware of the interrelationships among handicap, age, clothing, and adjustment; and gerontologists who should be advocates for the elderly and handicapped with respect to their broad, general needs.

This book can be important to clothing manufacturers since it will serve to call their attention to the many and diverse complexities of the needs of the aged and handicapped and the challenges these present when clothing is designed for their comfort and convenience as well as for attractiveness.

Finally, this book can be important to the aged and handicapped themselves since it speaks directly to them and should encourage them to consider their own needs and to know that so many experts in the various fields of human service and caring are turning their attention to these basic needs.

Doctor Adeline Hoffman, who has had a long-standing interest in the field of clothing for the elderly and handicapped, presents a thorough picture ranging from the history of the field to the most practical applications of the principles of both clothing and rehabilitation to solving the needs of an extremely diverse group of individuals. As she points out, the major problem has been one of neglect.

In a field which is still in its beginnings, this book should stimulate other students to direct their attention toward research and development in this and related areas. It is thus that we expand our knowledge so that we can teach better and serve better.

I take some personal pleasure in expressing my gratitude to Doctor Hoffman for her persistent, insightful, and thoughtful consideration of this important problem. We have been associated in various ways as colleague and friend for many years and I am pleased to commend this volume to the serious student.

WOODROW W. MORRIS, Ph.D.

INTRODUCTION

MOST people have very little difficulty in purchasing attractive, fashionable clothing in standard sizes that satisfy their personal and social needs, but for those who are physically handicapped, chronically ill, mentally retarded, or elderly, the problem of satisfying their clothing needs may be very difficult or impossible. The purpose of this book is to provide information on clothing for those with special needs. The book was written in response to the need and interest in this field as evidenced by continual requests for copies of workshop proceedings, bibliographies, reference sources, and course outlines by graduate students, health department officers, Extension Service Specialists, teachers of home economics in secondary schools, colleges, and universities, chain store personnel, and physically handicapped and aged individuals.

To provide some perspective in the field of special clothing needs, the developments which have taken place in the last three or four decades are briefly reviewed with emphasis on the most recent years. The text includes a description of handicaps which gives some measure of the magnitude of physical conditions that create clothing problems. Physical conditions which are not generally regarded as physical handicaps but do require special clothing are included.

Also considered is the psychological significance of clothing, not only in terms of social acceptability and self-image, but in terms of its therapeutic value and as a positive force in the rehabilitation process, especially where appearance and mobility have been adversely affected by physical handicaps or physical changes that may occur in the later years.

Clothing design problems are described in terms of those common to many kinds of physical limitations, particularly those which affect dressing and undressing and those which relate to the use of assistive devices such as crutches and wheelchairs, and some solutions are suggested. Though footwear is not classified as clothing, it is included in the text because of its importance in mobility problems of many physically handicapped and aged persons. Also included are dressing and grooming aids.

One of the problems common to all who have special clothing needs is where to find clothing to meet their needs. Sources briefly described in the book are custom-made garments, ready-made clothing adapted to special needs, and clothing made at home with patterns altered to meet individual needs. A number of illustrations appear in the book, but it is not within the scope of the book to provide complete detailed directions for adapting ready-made clothing and altering patterns for making clothing at home. Books on clothing construction provide such information with illustration of construction processes.

The book should be of special interest to home economists in the secondary schools, colleges, universities and Extension Service; directors of programs for the aged; administrators of mental retardation programs; rehabilitation specialists and counselors; nurses; social workers; nursing home directors; physical and occupational therapists; dressmakers and clothing designers; those who have personal responsibility for family members who have special clothing problems; and those who must find solutions to their own clothing problems.

In courses in clothing in home economics programs, special education, nursing, social work, physical and occupational therapy, and gerontology, the book may be especially useful as a reference.

In addition to the references at the end of each chapter, further literature appears in Appendix A, and a list of sources of clothing, footwear, and other special needs appears in Appendix B. National professional health related associations and others concerned with special clothing needs appear in Appendix C.

No book is ever complete, nor does writing remain up to date. Each day, someone discovers a new way to deal with a problem, and the ingenuity of those in need add to the total knowledge. Today's writers will be updated by tomorrow's writers in the continual march of progress as more people become interested and contribute to the body of knowledge in the field of special clothing. Leaders of yesterday laid the foundation on which we now build.

ACKNOWLEDGMENTS

THE information in the text comes from an accumulation from many sources over a period of years, including observation at hospitals, rehabilitation facilities, institutions for the mentally retarded, nursing homes, and residences for the aged. I also acknowledge, with thanks, the help of many people who were consulted in various areas of specialization at the University of Iowa College of Medicine and the University Hospitals, and elsewhere: Kathy Burds, Nursing Supervisor, General Surgery; Betty Dales, Clinical Nursing Specialist, Medical Nursing Division; Leo J. Morrisey, Assistant Professor, Educational Program in Physical Therapy; the late Dr. W. D. Paul, Professor Emeritus, Department of Orthopedic Surgery; Donald J. Shurr, Assistant Director for Patient Services, Department of Physical Therapy; Ruth Ann Small, Clinical Nursing Specialist, Urology Nursing Division; Jean Stoddard, Senior Physical Therapist, Iowa Burn Center; Martha Neuzil, Instructor in home economics, Iowa Braille and Sight Saving School: Norma Shepherd, County Coordinator, Reach to Recovery Program; Pauline Wright, Supervisor of Nursing; and Grace D. Young, Former Teacher of Home Economics, Hospital School for Severely Handicapped Children.

A.M.H.

CONTENTS

Clothing for the Handicapped the Aged, and Other People with Special Needs

Chapter 1

OVERVIEW

PRESENT concern for people in need is the greatest of any period of history. Our whole orientation to people in need is changing; there is a greater public awareness of need, an emerging social consciousness, a greater willingness to assume some responsibility and a feeling that "we are our brother's keeper."

In earlier times, the poor, the old, and the handicapped who could not be cared for within the immediate family were dependent on charity and were generally resigned to a fate of hopelessness. Severely handicapped and retarded children were not admitted to the public schools and were generally kept out of sight with no opportunity for emotional, intellectual, and social development and no opportunity to ever earn a living.

One major factor that has led to greater interest in special clothing needs has been the lengthened lifespan as a result of new developments in the field of medicine, and medical care and treatment. This has brought about the need for greater planning in terms of income, employment, quality of life, place in society and independence rather than dependence. Not only has there been effort to cure disease, keep people alive, and relieve limiting physical conditions, but there has been greater effort to maximize the potential of all people. A philosophy of possibilities has taken the place of the earlier acceptance of limitations. As the old, the physically handicapped, and mentally retarded take their places in society and work among other people, they must have clothing that is functional and attractive and that meets their special needs.

MODERN REHABILITATION

Rehabilitation of the physically handicapped and the development of special clothing to facilitate the activities of daily

living were two of the great pioneering efforts and achievements of Doctor Howard A. Rusk and his associates. Beginning
in the early 1940s in New York, this led to the establishment of
the Institute of Rehabilitation Medicine at the New York University Medical Center in 1948. These were the war years when
large numbers of disabled veterans were returning to the United
States, and it was the methods developed by Doctor Rusk and
his associates that brought about successful rehabilitation at
the Institute of Rehabilitation Medicine and which were later
used in other facilities in the United States and in many other
parts of the world. Known as the "father of modern rehabilitation," Doctor Rusk's philosophy was to treat the whole person
and to solve not only physical problems, but also emotional,
social, and psychological problems. He expressed his belief that
"people, fighting to regain their self-sufficiency and dignity,
have a depth of spirit that you and I know little about."[1]

In *Living With A Disability*,[2] written with Eugene J. Taylor,
Doctor Rusk devoted a whole chapter to clothing, and in his
later book, *A World To Care For*,[1] he tells the whole story of
his efforts in the field of rehabilitation of the physically handicapped from his initial work in 1942, in the Army-Air Force
Convalescent-Rehabilitation Program at the Jefferson Barracks
Hospital in Missouri, to the present time at the Institute of
Rehabilitation Medicine at the New York University Medical
Center. It was largely through Doctor Rusk's efforts that physical medicine and rehabilitation was officially recognized as
one of the medical specialties by the American Medical Association in 1947.

New Life For Millions, by Russell J. N. Dean,[3] tells the story
of the great leaders of the twentieth century in the field of
rehabilitation "who gave us today's often miraculous programs
for rescuing seriously disabled people from oblivion." His
seventy-year rehabilitation "Hall of Fame" includes, in addition to Doctor Rusk, Jeremiah Milbank, John A. Kratz, Doctor
Henry H. Kessler, Doctor Frank H. Krusen, and Mary E.
Switzer.

Following physical rehabilitation, vocational rehabilitation
provided training for employment of the physically handi-

capped; in 1945, the National Employ the Physically Handicapped Week was inaugurated, followed in 1947 by the organization of the President's Committee on Employment of the Physically Handicapped, which brought forth much cooperation from leaders in business, industry, labor, veteran's affairs, and medicine. This was the beginning of a continuous program of public education and promotion concerned with employment opportunities for all handicapped people. In 1963, the President's Committee on Mental Retardation came into being and the mentally retarded were added to the President's Committee on Employment of the Physically Handicapped by removing the word "physically."[3]

While employment was bringing economic independence and greater social acceptance to large numbers of the handicapped, it was the Rehabilitation Act of 1973 and its later amendments that provided for the removal of architectural barriers from public buildings, recreational and educational facilities, and public transportation. With the removal of these barriers, many more of the physically handicapped came into view, which brought about further need for special clothing designed to minimize appearance of physical handicaps and add to the further social acceptance of people with physical handicaps. The *Education for All Handicapped Children Act of 1975*, requiring "free appropriate public education" for all handicapped children including the physically handicapped and mentally retarded, will bring into view many children who had been in institutions, special schools, and at home.[4] This will bring about the need not only for clothing adapted to physical conditions and mental limitations but also for clothing that will make handicapped children look more like nonhandicapped children.

One of the earliest efforts on behalf of the physically handicapped took place before the turn of the century and was the forerunner of one of the best known sources of clothing for those with special needs. The "Sunbeam Circle," formed by a group of Cleveland school girls to help bedfast children in a ward at the old Lakeside Hospital, progressed to the establishment of a kindergarten for crippled children and then to special

education classes. Following a series of changes and developments spanning more than a half century, the Vocational
Guidance and Rehabilitation Services of Cleveland came into
being and has pioneered in the field of clothing for the physically handicapped.[3] Clothing is one of the means of removing
attitudinal barriers by making those likely to be rejected more
attractive and socially acceptable.

THE AGED

The aged have come into focus largely because of the lengthening span of life and the increase in numbers, both absolute
and relative, since the beginning of the century. Before the
twentieth century, there was no systematic study of aging in the
United States. By 1940, gerontology (the study of aging) came
into its own, and in 1945, the Gerontological Society was organized. The first national conference on aging was called by
President Truman in 1950, and in 1956, the Special Staff on
Aging was established in the Department of Health, Education
and Welfare. In 1962, the President's Council on Aging was
organized, on which all departments of government were represented. The *Older Americans Act of 1965* established a new
framework for expression of federal responsibility in the field
of aging, and as a result, the Administration on Aging was
established in the Department of Health, Education and Welfare.

White House conferences on aging were convened in 1961
and 1971, and in 1974, the National Institute on Aging was
established in the National Institutes of Health. The statement
of mission declares that "The National Institute on Aging was
established for the conduct and support of biomedical, social
and behavioral research and training related to the aging process, diseases and other special problems of the aged."[5] The
motivation of Congress in establishing the Institute was that
"in addition to the physical infirmities resulting from advanced
age, the economic, social and psychological factors associated
with aging operate to exclude millions of older Americans from
the full life and a place in our society to which their years of

service and experience entitle them."[5]

Housing and living arrangements of many older people have changed as families and housing have grown smaller and as frequent changes in place of residence of the younger generation have become more common. As a result of these changes, most older people no longer live with their children, and housing for older people has become a proper public function. For older couples and individuals living alone, there is need for ego support, for social relationships and a role in society. Clothing must serve not only needs related to physical conditions among the aged but also needs of a social and psychological nature.

Clothing is one of the essential needs of all people and is a subject of universal interest. Beginning in the late nineteenth century, psychologists, sociologists, and anthropologists engaged in study of the social significance of clothing, but it has been only in the last four or five decades that occupational therapists, physical therapists, apparel designers, and home economists have applied their knowledge of design, construction, and the social significance of clothing to the special clothing needs of people, particularly the physically handicapped and the aged.

REFERENCES

1. Rusk, Howard A.: *A World To Care For*. New York, Random, 1972.
2. Rusk, Howard A. and Taylor, Eugene J.: *Living With A Disability*. New York, Blakiston, 1953.
3. Dean, Russell J. N.: *New Life For Millions*. New York, Hastings, 1972.
4. *Key Federal Regulations Affecting the Handicapped 1975-76*. Washington, DC, U S Government Printing Office, 1977.
5. *National Institute on Aging*. DHEW Publication No. (NIH) 76-1129, National Institute on Aging, National Institutes on Health. Washington, DC, 1976.

Chapter 2

ORIGIN, INCIDENCE, AND
DESCRIPTION OF HANDICAPS

HANDICAP is a term that can refer to a broad range of conditions of life, some of which are readily evident and others hardly visible. Handicaps may be social, cultural, educational, psychological, financial, mental, and physical. Many people are physically handicapped in one way or another, but society does not regard them as handicapped if the handicap is not visible. A physical handicap may be defined as inability to function normally without some kind of help. The terms handicap and disability are often used synonymously; however, disability refers to a condition of physical impairment which results in a handicap. Wright describes handicap as the "cumulative result of the obstacles which disability interpose between the individual and his maximum functional level."[1]

Most handicaps are a matter of degreee rather than only of kind. Among the physical handicaps that are largely taken for granted are sight limitations that require the use of glasses of some kind, auditory limitations that require the use of hearing aids, and the loss of teeth that require the use of artificial dentures. The physical handicaps that bring about the need for special clothing are those that involve the total or partial loss of control of joints and muscles in the hands, arms, legs, feet, neck, shoulders, and back; loss of bladder and bowel control; loss of ability to stand, walk, and balance; and also amputation of the upper and lower extremities.

ORIGIN OF PHYSICAL HANDICAPS

The origin of physical handicaps may be classified under the three broad headings of, (1) birth defects, (2) diseases, and (3) accidents. In addition to these, physical conditions may develop soon after birth or at a later time in life which cannot be classified as diseases and do not result from accidents.

Birth Defects

Among the birth defects of highest incidence are cerebral palsy, muscular dystrophy, malformation of limbs, spina bifida, scoliosis, and other physical deformities. Multiple sclerosis also may be regarded as a birth defect though it does not make its initial appearance until early adulthood or at a later time in life. Blindness may also be a birth defect or may occur at a later time in life.

Cerebral Palsy

This is a general term applied to a group of permanently disabling symptoms resulting from nonprogressive damage to the developing brain. It may occur before birth, during birth, or after birth but is generally classified as a birth defect. The major characteristic is loss or impairment of control of voluntary muscles. Motor involvements include awkward or involuntary movements, tightness of muscles, poor balance, and irregular gait, which often result in falling, so the use of protective helmets becomes necessary to avoid head injuries. Though cerebral palsy is a neurological condition, it is frequently accompanied by other handicaps including mental retardation, poorly articulated speech, convulsions, visual disorders, hearing impairment, shortening of extremities, learning disabilities, behavioral disorders, and contraction of joints fixed in awkward positions.[2,3]

The five major types of cerebral palsy are (1) spastic, in which there are muscle spasms and which is the most frequently occurring motor symptom of cerebral palsy, (2) athetosis, which is marked by constantly recurring, slow, involuntary writhing movements of the arms and legs, (3) ataxia, in which there is incoordination and inability or awkwardness in maintaining balance, (4) tremor, in which there is tremulous action similar to the tremulousness as seen in adults who have Parkinson's disease, and (5) rigidity, in which muscles contract slowly and stiffly, leading to clumsiness. It is estimated that 750,000 to 1,000,000 persons have cerebral palsy and that about 15,000 babies are born with cerebral palsy per year or as many as one in every 200 live births.[2,3]

Muscular Dystrophy

This is a chronic, progressive disease characterized by wasting and consequent weakness of voluntary muscles. As weakness increases, patients are confined to wheelchairs and eventually to bed. Symptoms of muscular dystrophy in children are frequent falling, difficulty in ascending stairs, a waddling gait, difficulty in raising from a lying or sitting position to a standing position, and contractures leading to distortions of the affected muscles. Weakness in the shoulder girdle and upper arms is noted during adolescence and the lower limbs are also affected. In adults, the earliest muscles affected are those of the shoulders, upper arms, thighs, and back. It is estimated that there are more than 200,000 men, women and children who have muscular dystrophy and that about two-thirds of them are children between the ages of three and thirteen years. Since muscular dystrophy is not currently reportable, a national census has not been taken and all incidence figures are estimates.[2,3]

There are several types of muscular dystrophy based on hereditary patterns, onset, muscular involvement and progression. The most prevalent type is pseudohypertrophic, which commences in childhood between the ages of two and ten years, or soon after birth, and its course is more rapid than the other types. Death usually occurs within ten to fifteen years after onset, though some patients survive considerably longer. The juvenile type commences anywhere from the first to the third decade of life, with variable progression, but slower than the most prevalent type and patients usually live to middleage or longer. The facio-scapulohumeral type commences in early adolescence and young adulthood and affects the shoulders and upper arms, making it very difficult to raise the arms above the head. Progression in this type is slow and the average lifespan is rarely shortened though patients may suffer considerable disability.[2]

Spina Bifida

This is a birth defect that literally means "cleft spine." In Latin, *bifidus* means split into two parts and refers to a failure of the two sides of the developing spinal cord to come together completely, leaving a cleft or defect in the spinal canal. In its slightest form, called *spinal bifida occulta*, meaning hidden below the skin, this abnormality causes no symptoms and may never be discovered except through x-rays which are taken for some other purpose.

In a more serious form of spina bifida, a sac as small as a nut or as large as a grapefruit protrudes from the backbone, usually at the lower end of the spine. At birth, the sac is sometimes completely covered with skin, but in other cases, the nerve tissue is exposed. Since the sac most commonly contains portions of the lower end of the spinal cord, it is the legs of the patient which are most likely to be affected.[4]

In mild forms, the only difficulty might be weak muscles and inadequate skin sensation. If the injury to the spinal cord is more serious, the patient could have leg paralysis and no skin sensation on the legs. Even in relatively mild spina bifida, bladder and bowel control is likely to be a troublesome complication. Such symptoms are ordinarily present at birth or may develop for the first time during adolescence. Because of the paralysis of some muscles in the legs, it is common for patients to develop stiffening of the joints and abnormalities of posture of the legs and feet, which may require corrective shoes, braces, crutches and other devices.[4]

In the most severe form of spina bifida, involving a twisted spine, dislocated hips or misshapen pelvis, and lack of bladder and bowel control, an infant may live only a very short time.

As in other birth defects, the cause of spina bifida is unknown. Estimates of the incidence of spina bifida are difficult to make since this condition occurs with other abnormalities and may be classified under one of the others, or may be included under the general classification of birth abnormalities. The estimated number of new cases per year is about 3 for every 1,000 live births. Based on this rate, it is estimated that 11,000 children are born with this birth defect every year. Deaths from spina bifida are estimated at 1,151 every year. However, the survival rate among children with spina bifida is increasing as a result of research in surgery and medical and nursing care.[4]

Scoliosis

Scoliosis literally means a condition of crookedness and is composed of the Greek words *skolios*, meaning bent or crooked, plus the suffix *osis*, denoting a condition of. It is an ancient term which was used by Hippocrates for any type of curvature. However, modern usage now restricts the term scoliosis to designate a lateral curvature of the spine. Though abnormal, such curvature is common and can be caused by a variety of physical conditions.[5]

Functional scoliosis is a lateral curvature of the spine caused by poor posture or a short leg and can be corrected by the efforts of the child. It does not usually lead to serious consequences. Structural scoliosis, however, cannot be corrected by the child and can lead to serious deformities. It may be congenital or be caused by neuromuscular abnormalities, or the cause may remain unknown. In congenital scoliosis, there may be abnormalities in the formation or segmentation of the bones in the spine which can produce serious deformities and may require surgery. One form of scoliosis is associated with a condition known as neurofibromatosis, in which the scoliosis can progress rapidly and create severe deformities with pressure on the spinal cord. This is often accompanied by weakness of the muscles and interruption of body functions below the level of pressure on the spinal cord.[2, 6]

Scoliosis of unknown origin sometimes appears in early adolescence during a period of rapid growth. This form of scoliosis, which is painless, shows up in the unequal height of the shoulders or the pelvis. Diagnosis is made by x-ray and treatment depends on the severity of the deformity and the likelihood of progressive deformity. In very severe cases, surgery is performed, and in many cases a Milwaukee brace is required. This type of brace is conspicuous, consisting of a part that fits around the pelvis which is connected both at the back and at the front of the body, with a part that fits around the upper part of the neck against the base of the head and under the chin. Clothing worn over a Milwaukee brace requires some adaptation concerned mainly with fitting and appearance, but also with abrasion resistance.[2, 6]

There are no recent accurate figures for the incidence of scoliosis in the United States. However, two doctors made a survey of scoliosis prevalance in Minnesota and reported there are about 1.3 per thousand in the adolescent population who have scoliosis requiring referral to an orthopedist, and that many more females are affected than males.[7]

Mental Retardation

Mental retardation is a condition, often congenital, in which normal development fails to take place as the infant grows older. Mental retardation should not be confused with mental illness, which is a breakdown of normal brain functioning, resulting in disorders of behavior, mood, and thought, and which may occur at almost any age in previously mentally normal people. It is estimated that 6 million Americans are mentally retarded and the impact of mental retardation is directly felt by 20 million family members who share the burden and problems of care of the retarded, whose inadequate intellectual development impairs their ability to learn and to adapt to the demands of society. An estimated 126,000 children are born each year who will be diagnosed as mentally retarded.[1, 2]

The most common figure used to specify the number of retarded persons within a given population at a given point in time is 3 percent.[8] Mental retardation is a problem of great magnitude and may be considered to be the most handicapping of all childhood disorders. In addition to those accounted for in the statistics of the mentally retarded, there are many who function ineffectively during a whole lifetime but are not identified and included in the statistics.[3]

There is no single cause of mental retardation but there are many known causes, and there are numerous cases of mental retardation in which the cause remains unknown. Mental retardation results when there is (1) incomplete development or destruction of tissues of the central nervous system, (2) lack of brain development before birth, (3) genetic-metabolic diseases, (4) chromosomal disorders, (5) certain illnesses, infections, and glandular disorders during pregnancy, (6) extraordinarily prolonged labor or pelvic pressure, hemorrhage, or lack of oxygen during pregnancy or delivery, any of which may injure the child's brain, (7) accident, poisoning, glandular disturbance, chemical imbalance, or childhood disease, and (8) premature birth and cerebral palsy. Recent research also points to severe early emotional deprivation and other cultural and environmental factors as causes of mental retardation.[2] In this chapter, however, it is classified as a birth defect. There are many systems used to classify the mentally retarded for specific purposes. The legal-administrative classification system regulates who is eligible for services for the mentally retarded and the educational classification system divides them into three groups, on the basis of their ability to respond to education, as educable, trainable, and custodial.[3]

The classification according to intelligence, which was developed by the American Association of Mental Deficiency, is based on a series of tests. The levels of retardation according to intellectual functioning are profound, severe, moderate, and mild retardation. Those in the profound group are completely dependent, are in need of constant care, and have physical handicaps such as lack of coordination and sensory development in addition to their mental retardation. Those in the severe group are able to move about by themselves, and though they are not completely dependent, they also have some physical handicaps and need constant care. The moderately retarded group includes the "trainables" or those who lack mental development but are able to care for themselves. In the mildly retarded group, children are slow in developing but are able to learn within limits; adults in this group can be given job training and can live independently. The mentally retarded, in general, may have a short attention span and problems of visual-motor association and visual perceptual functioning in addition to limitations in ability to learn and in speed of learning.[8] Clothing needs are largely those related to dressing and undressing and to deviant behavior.

DISEASES AND SOME OTHER PHYSICAL CONDITIONS

Some physical handicaps are described as both diseases and as physical conditions because their origin is unknown. Among these diseases and physical conditions that affect large numbers of people are arthritis, multiple sclerosis, hemiplegia, and amputations of upper and lower extremities.

Arthritis and the Rheumatic Diseases

These diseases are second only to heart disease as the most widespread of chronic illnesses in the United States. Arthritis is inflamation of a joint, marked by pain, heat, redness, swelling, and deformity. The term arthritis, which is composed of the Greek words *artheron* or joint and *itis* or inflamation, is sometimes used to cover a wide range of pathological conditions. Among the major forms of arthritis are rheumatoid arthritis and osteoarthritis. Rheumatoid is the most crippling form of arthritis and is a chronic inflamatory connective tissue disease that leads to permanent joint deformities and other complications producing disabilities and chronic invalidism, affecting people of all ages from young adults to those in the later years of life. More than 5 million people in the United States have rheumatic arthritis.[2]

Osteoarthritis is another form of arthritis which is degeneration of joint tissues and which is associated with aging. Though it develops more slowly than rheumatic arthritis, is milder, and less painful, it can finally produce much pain and disability. More than 10 million people in the United States have this form of arthritis. This form of arthritis brings about limitations in the grasp and range of motions of the hands and arms.[2]

Multiple Sclerosis

Multiple sclerosis is a chronic, progressive, and crippling neurological disease which makes its initial appearance between the ages of twenty to forty years. It is characterized by relatively short periods of increasing disability followed by much longer periods of stability or improvement, but its cause remains unknown. It is slow and incidious in onset and difficult to diagnose until symptoms have progressed to the point of disability. Among the symptoms of multiple sclerosis are double vision, staggering and inability to keep one's balance, numbness or paralysis of parts of the body, tremor, involuntary movements of the eyeballs, extreme weakness in the lower limbs, speech difficulties, and bladder and bowel difficulties.[2]

It is estimated that over 500,000 people in the United States have multiple sclerosis and related diseases. As stated by leading neurologists, multiple sclerosis is one of the leading cripplers of young adults in the United States with 70 percent of all patients first diagnosed between the ages of 20 and 40 years, fifteen percent between the ages of 15 and 20 years, and 15 percent between 40 and 50 years. While concentrated among young adults, the chronic and progressive nature of this crippling disease makes it a significant problem among older people. One of the problems in making reasonably accurate estimates of the incidence of multiple sclerosis is that this disease is difficult to diagnose in its early stages, so new cases may be easily omitted from surveys.[2]

Hemiplegia

Hemiplegia, commonly called "stroke," is the result of a cerebral vascular accident. It is not a disease, but a paralysis of one side of the body.[9] Hemiplegia comes from the Greek words *hemi* or half and *plegis* or strike, and describes a one-sided paralysis. It is the result of a condition that affects the arterial blood supply to the brain and may be caused by a variety of pathological situations. Though it frequently occurs in people in the best of health, medical history of stroke patients usually shows that many have had pre-existing hypertension or high blood pressure.[10] Damage to the brain is on the side opposite the paralysis, so a person with a lesion of the left cerebral hemisphere will incur a right-sided hemiplegia or right-sided paralysis, and a person with a lesion of the right cerebral hemisphere will incur a left-sided paralysis. If paralysis is not total, it is called *paresis* or *hemiparesis,* which means weakness or partial paralysis on one side of the body.[9] Those with a lesion on the left may have speech problems or aphasia, which may also include reading and writing, and those with a lesion on the right may be subject to perceptual and cognitive problems which will involve the areas of dressing because they will not be able to interpret shapes and forms of once-familiar objects.[10]

Hemiplegia affects voluntary control of both the arms and the legs; contractures occur which tend to create a stance with the paralyzed arm flexed at the elbow, wrist, and fingers, the shoulders and lower extremities rotated inward toward the middle of the body, and the knees and ankles flexed. In addition, there may be less response to touch, temperature, and pain on the affected side. In typical cases, a patient will have some return of motor power in the lower extremity, while the upper extremity may remain useless, but all combinations are possible; there could also be some incoordination which would interfere with the process of dressing. Stroke is considered the most prevalent crippler in the United States and it is estimated that about 1.5 million are disabled by it to some degree each year. Stroke or hemiplegia occurs at all ages, however, most often at birth, in the middle years, and in old age. At birth, it is classified as one of the forms of cerebral palsy. The greatest incidence is in people over fifty years of age.[9] For hemiplegia victims, clothing must be adapted for ease in dressing and undressing.

Amputation

Amputation is a disability that may affect children, adults, and aged persons, since it may occur at any time during the lifespan. It may be congenital or a result of disease or injury. The youngest in chronological occurrence is in the infant born a congenital amputee with an incomplete extremity or extremities, and the oldest is the elderly person who must have surgical amputation because of diabetes or a gangrenous condition. Estimated incidence of amputation among those from birth to sixteen years of age is over 25,000.[9]

Among amputees up to four or five years of age, nearly all are congenital, and from age six to sixteen, approximately 75 percent are congenital. In this age group, many are affected by injuries and few by surgical removal due to disease. Child amputees are sometimes classified under malformations of extremities rather than congenital amputees. For adults, ages seventeen to fifty-five years, the estimated incidence is 175,000, with three times as many male as female amputees. Of this number, about 75 percent are due to injuries caused by accidents and war, and a significant number are caused by disease, particularly cancer. In this age group, there are approximately three and one-half times as many lower as upper extremity amputees. In the over fifty-five-year age-group, there are about 200,000 amputees, in which practically all new amputations are due to disease, especially diabetes and cardiovascular conditions.[9]

Amputees can be described in terms of the number of extremities affected as unilateral (one side affected) or bilateral (both sides affected), single, double (two extremities affected), or multiple (more than two extremities affected). The amount of physical function potentially restorable to the unilateral amputee is related to the number of joints that have been lost, and in general, as the number of joints lost increases, the extent of functional restoration possible decreases significantly, and as the number of limb amputations increases, functional potential decreases drastically. Following amputation surgery, there are chronic medical problems that continue indefinitely which require intermittent medical and prosthetic care throughout the individual's lifetime. Among the problems are contractions of stump muscles, neuramata and scar tissue (that cause discomfort and pain), excessive perspiration and skin irritation (due to pressure), and circulatory deficiencies. These problems are more serious for lower extremities than for upper extremities because of the weight-bearing function.[9]

Accidents

Accidents cause injuries of all degrees of severity. Among the most severe are spinal cord injuries which affect motion and control of joints and muscles and result in some degree of paralysis. The two basic types of paralysis are paraplegia which affects the lower extremities, and quadriplegia, which affects all four extremities." In paraplegia, the injury occurs in the lumbar spine; in quadriplegia, the injury occurs in the cervical spine. In addition to injuries that result from accidents, these spinal cord conditions can be caused by congenital abnormalities such as cerebral palsy, muscular dystrophy, spina bifida and disorders such as multiple sclerosis and poliomyelitis. When caused by injuries, they are called traumatic paraplegia and quadriplegia. Such injuries are results of motor vehicle accidents, sports accidents (especially diving and skiing), industrial accidents which include falls and damage from heavy machinery and equipment, and bullet wounds. The greatest source of injuries, among young people, are those caused by motor vehicle accidents.[10]

In spinal cord injuries, the paralysis is caused by interruptions of the nerve pathways and pathways from the brain to the involved extremities. These pathways are located in the spinal cord which goes through the vertebra that makes up the spinal column. Spinal cord pathways that have been torn apart do not grow together, with the result that paralysis becomes permanent. In addition to the paralysis, the function of the bowels and bladder are affected. Rehabilitation of those with spinal cord injuries is successful and they do return to normal life, but the function of the paralyzed extremities cannot be restored. Thus they live with the limitations imposed by the use of braces, crutches, and wheelchairs. These are not reportable conditions, so the exact number is not known, but it has been estimated by the Department of Health, Education and Welfare that there are now over 200,000 people who are disabled by spinal cord injuries and who are paralyzed to some extent. More than three-fourths of those affected are males, whose activities in sports, industry, and the use of motor vehicles makes them more prone to accidents.[6, 9]

REFERENCES

1. Wright, Beatrice A.: *Physical Disability — A Psychological Approach.* New York, Har-Row, 1960.
2. *Facts on the Major Killing and Crippling Diseases in the United States.* National Health Education Committee. United Nations Plaza, New York, 1971.
3. *The Killers and Cripplers — Facts on Major Diseases in the United States Today.* National Health Education Committee. New York, McKay, 1976.
4. *SPINA BIFIDA — A Birth Defect.* DHEW Publication No. (NIH) 72-309. National Institutes of Neurological Diseases and Stroke, National Institutes of Health, Bethesda, Maryland, 1972.
5. Wain, Harry: *The Story Behind the Word — Some Interesting Origins of Medical Terms.* Springfield, Thomas, 1958.
6. Bleck, Eugene and Nagel, Donald A.: *Physically Handicapped Children — A Manual for Teachers.* New York, Grune, 1975.
7. Kane, William J. and Moe, John H.: A scoliosis-prevalence survey in Minnesota. *Clinical Orthopaedics and Related Research, 69*:216-218, March-April, 1970.
8. Browning, Philip L. (Ed.): *Mental Retardation: Rehabilitation and Counseling.* Springfield, Thomas, 1974.
9. Garrett, James F. and Levine, Edna S. (Eds.): *Psychological Practices With the Physically Disabled.* New York, Columbia U Pr, 1973.
10. Bonner, Charles D.: *Medical Care and Rehabilitation of the Aged and Chronically Ill.* Boston, Little, 1974.

Chapter 3

RECENT AND CURRENT EFFORTS
TO SATISFY CLOTHING NEEDS

As the members of the medical profession and
the social scientists became more interested in the needs of the
physically handicapped and the aged in the 1940s, other professional groups concerned themselves with the clothing needs of
the physically handicapped and the aged, and others with special needs. Historically, however, society had taken little or no
interest in these minority groups.

The physically handicapped and the deformed were isolated
from society by attitudes of people who believed that they were
helpless, hopeless, unworthy of attention, and of no use to society. They were either kept at home and generally out of sight
or were institutionalized where their physical needs were taken
care of, but no consideration was given to their social and
psychological needs and to the possibility of their rehabilitation and their normal functioning in society. The span of life
for the physically handicapped was shorter because little or no
effort was made at rehabilitation. Surgery and medical care was
limited compared to the present, and fewer persons recovered
from diseases and injuries resulting from accidents.

Clothing, for those with special needs, was probably ready-
made and altered or adapted for them according to the interest,
ability, and ingenuity of family members and others who were
responsible for them, but no clothing was designed and made
available for those with special needs. Clothing was of very
little concern, and it was not until the 1940s that articles began
to appear in the literature on clothing needs and problems of
dressing and undressing. Attitudes toward all people in need,
including the physically handicapped, the aged, the chronically
ill, and the mentally retarded, have undergone much change
during the last three or four decades and the terms *human*

values, human needs, human relationships, and *human rights* are now very much within the common vocabulary. Society now places some value on all individuals and is concerned with their dignity, independence, and quality of life.

CLOTHING FOR PHYSICALLY HANDICAPPED CHILDREN

Much of the early work on clothing for physically handicapped children was done by occupational therapists, because they were among the first to come into contact with children in need. Dressing and undressing was assigned to occupational therapists because it was a preliminary step toward getting patients into occupational therapy activities. Occupational therapy became highly specialized in dressing and undressing techniques through analysis of motions and the learning process. In the early 1930s, aspects of dressing and undressing were incorporated into the treatment programs in hospitals and clinics as part of the care of children, especially those with cerebral palsy.

In the early 1940s, there was a change in philosophy, from caring for people and keeping them comfortable to making them independent and responsible for themselves. Later in the 1940s, normal child development, studied by Doctor Arthur Gesell and his associates, included the dressing sequence of normal children; the findings were of help to therapists concerned with physical limitations.

By the 1950s, charts on dressing abilities of normal children were used by therapists in teaching handicapped children. Those working with cerebral palsied children in New York raised questions about the lack of practical clothing and this led some physical therapists, notably Mary Eleanor Brown, to develop some clothing to fill the needs. The work of Mary Eleanor Brown was based on her experience as a pupil and a "little teacher" in her mother's Montessori School which opened in 1912. The impact of sensorial training and daily activity emphasis led to her extensive work, from the early 1940s to the 1950s, in developing in handicapped children the skills of dressing and undressing.[1]

A news story in the *New York Herald Tribune* in the late

1950s reported that —

> Miss Brown has designed, in collaboration with other physical therapists, under medical supervision, a collection of clothes for handicapped youngsters that are easy to get into and out of, attractive and often of great psychological importance. "Few people realize it," says Miss Brown, "but dressing and undressing involve a very complex set of motions. They're among the most complicated things we do in daily life."[2]

Outstanding among her many publications is her chapter on "Self-help clothing" in *Orthotics* (1966).

Home economists were also interested in self-help features in children's clothing to facilitate the training of normal children in dressing and undressing. In 1956, an article entitled "Dress design with self-help features for the pre-school child," by Eleanor Boettke and Margaret Zook, appeared in the *Journal of Home Economics* based on the graduate research of Eleanor Boettke. Following her graduate program at the Pennsylvania State University, she joined the faculty of the School of Home Economics at the University of Connecticut and, in 1955, engaged in a project on "Work Simplification in the Area of Child Care for Physically Handicapped Women." Two years later, she published the results in a bulletin entitled "Suggestions for Physically Handicapped Mothers on Clothing for Pre-School Children." This led to a collaborative project by the School of Home Economics at the university, the Hartford Rehabilitation Center, and the Connecticut Society for Crippled Children and Adults, the cost of which was covered by a grant from the Zeta Tau Alpha fraternity for women. The results of the project appeared in the publication of the National Society of Crippled Children and Adults in 1962 (entitled "Self-help clothing for handicapped children," co-authored by Clari Bare, Eleanor Boettke, and Neva Waggoner) and was the most definitive work in this area at that time.

CLOTHING FOR PHYSICALLY HANDICAPPED ADULTS

In the field of specially designed clothing for physically handicapped adults, the Institute of Physical Medicine and

Rehabilitation, at the New York University Medical Center in New York City, played a major role. Beginning in 1950, adaptation of clothing and special devices to assist in dressing became a part of the program of the Institute of Physical Medicine and Rehabilitation. A study was made in the early 1950s on self-help devices for the purpose of making accumulated information generally available to those in need. Funded by a grant from the National Foundation for Infantile Paralysis, the "Self-Help Device Research Project" was directed by Doctor Howard A. Rusk and Eugene Taylor in collaboration with Muriel Zimmerman, O.T.R., and Julia Judson, M.S. At the same time, another research project was initiated in cooperation with the Disabled Homemakers Research Fund, which was established by a number of the leading public utility companies, and the results of both projects were reported in *Living With a Disability*,[3] which included a chapter on clothing and self-help dressing devices.

Efforts in this direction, however, were limited until 1955, when the services of the late Helen Cookman were enlisted. A highly experienced and well-recognized designer, Helen Cookman directed her expertise toward the solution of some of the problems of adults who still had dressing problems when they were discharged from the Institute. She explained:

> For many years, we've taken care of everyone in our population with special needs. We've made clothes for active sports and for maternity wear; we've produced work uniforms and proportioned-fit for the short, the tall, and the overweight. But strangely enough, nothing had ever been done for the nation's disabled, a total of five or six million people in the United States who use braces, crutches and whose clothes must be easy to manage.
>
> It was hard to know where to start, but there was no doubt about our objective — to make a handicapped person look as well dressed as anyone else, and to invent closings that would enable the handicapped to dress themselves with no help, or a minimum of help, according to the degree of disability. To me, that meant functional cut with a maximum of eye appeal, classic clothes that would be timeless and economical to manufacture.[4]

Limited experimentation led to a pilot project for which Helen Cookman served as coordinator and Muriel Zimmerman and others worked with Mrs. Cookman. In the course of their work, a non-profit corporation, Clothing Research, Inc., was formed for the purpose of conducting a market survey of functional fashions for the physically handicapped. In the pilot project, seventeen clothing items were developed and were tested prior to manufacture. The seventeen models were publicly presented at a national convention of occupational therapists in 1959 and were publicized in 600 newspaper articles both here and abroad, which brought forth requests for further information and inquiries from 35,000 individuals and 700 organizations. A grant from the Office of Vocational Rehabilitation supported further development of the program and in the early 1960s, the Clothing Research and Development Foundation was established as a nonprofit independent organization, working closely with the Institute and other rehabilitation organizations.[5]

Many individuals and groups, seeking to manufacture and distribute clothing for the physically handicapped, have experienced some disappointment in finding that this particular market is difficult to identify and to reach, and possibly not as large as was anticipated in relation to the whole market. The manufacturing and distribution of garments designed by Helen Cookman did not move as well as had been anticipated. They had hoped that the project would eventually include all basic garments for men, women and children. However, it was found that no mass market existed for garments designed for the physically handicapped though a few high fashion designers did produce some garments with a "functional fashion" label, using Helen Cookman's designs. As a result of a three-year study, "Functional Fashions for the Physically Handicapped" was published by the Institute in 1961 and provided much helpful information which was not available from any other source at that time.[5]

Clothing had always been one of the areas of interest of the Agricultural Research Service of the U.S. Department of Agriculture, and in 1959, Clarice Scott, then Clothing Specialist, reported the results of a survey she made of seventy handicapped homemakers in Washington, D.C., concerning the kind of clothing they wore and their clothing likes and dislikes. The handicaps represented among the seventy women included arthritis, muscular dystrophy, multiple sclerosis, poliomyelitis, amputations, and injuries from accidents. The findings from the study appeared in an article in the *Journal of Home Economics* in 1959 entitled "Clothing Needs of the Physically Handicapped," and in a bulletin of the Agricultural Research Service in 1961 entitled "Clothes for the Physically Handicapped with Features Suitable for All Women." The bulletin contained designs for about twenty women's clothing items together with photographs of the modeled garments and details on construction processes used. At the time the bulletin was published, some patterns for the garments were made available.[5]

In the early 1960s, Extension Clothing Specialists and County Extension Home Economists began to include in their programs assistance to physically handicapped individuals in the area of special clothing needs. A report[6] to the State College Committee of the Governor's Committee for the Handicapped (by Bernice Tharp, Extension Clothing Specialist, Pennsylvania State University) described the work of County Extension Home Economists in the field of clothing needs of physically handicapped individuals as revealed in their 1961 and 1962 annual reports. In her report, she referred to a statement made in 1962 by the Director of Home Economics Programs, Federal Extension Service, informing all State Home Economics Extension Leaders that "staff members of the Bureau of Family Services, Social Security Administration, Department of Health, Education and Welfare, have discussed with us the possibility of Extension Home Economists cooperating with state and local public assistance agencies in helping the physically handicapped, especially with clothing problems, work simplification and nutrition. As you know, such work is presently being done by agents and specialists in several areas of the country." Some states have developed extensive programs in this field and have published bulletins to provide the needed information.[6]

Also in the 1960s and continuing to the present time, the American Home Economics Association has indicated its interest in the area of clothing needs of the physically handicapped through articles in the *Journal of Home Economics* and featured speakers at the annual conventions. In 1968, the American Home Economics Association offered a series of one-day visits to a number of rehabilitation centers for home economists interested in graduate programs in rehabilitation, funded by a grant from the Rehabilitation Services Administration under the AHEA-RSA Traineeship Program. These visits included observation and discussion of clothing and dressing aids.

Some individuals, who suddenly find themselves with physical disabilities of their own, become aware of other people who have similar disabilities and, therefore, essentially the same needs. This was the experience of Mrs. Van Davis Odell, founder of Fashion-Able, who had a cerebral aneurysm which left her paralyzed on her left side. When she found that she could no longer get in and out of the usual undergarments, she was very surprised and disappointed to discover that there were no brands on the market that would satisfy her special needs. She relates that her decision to do something about filling this rehabilitation vacuum followed the chance reading of a magazine article about a one-handed mother. The article stated that there were more than 11,000,000 physically handicapped women in this country at that time, and she thought that if she could restore independent dressing for even a fraction of them, she could find no better way to occupy her time.[7]

Though Mrs. Odell had never been a designer, she had spent most of her business life in advertising and promotion of textiles and apparel, so she put her experience to good use. At the time she started to make undergarments for physically handicapped women, she found that there was absolutely no marketing data available as to the whereabouts of the physically handicapped women or their needs, so she started in a small way, concentrating on those dressing problems she knew best.

As Fashion-Able grew in volume, she added other items. The business was incorporated in New York in 1965 and a few years later, following the retirement of her husband, they moved to Florida. In 1971, the business had grown so large that the Odells were no longer able to handle it themselves and they sold the business to the R. D. Hardestys, long time friends in Rocky Hills, New Jersey, where the business is now located. Over the years, the business has expanded to include a full line of garments for physically handicapped women and other items needed in the activities of daily living for physically handicapped persons.[7]

The development of specially designed clothing for the physically handicapped and the mentally retarded, at the Vocational Guidance and Rehabilitation Services of Cleveland, Ohio, in 1962, marked an important milestone in dealing with clothing problems. Olive K. Bannister was then the Executive Director and Dorothy Behrens was the Director of Special Clothing Design and Head of the Sewing Department. In response to requests from nursing home administrators in the Cleveland area, Mrs. Behrens designed and made a dress for elderly women patients so they would not always have to wear hospital-type gowns. The dress was a back-wrapper style, designed to cope with many problems; following its success, Mrs. Behrens designed and made a back-opening slip to go with it. Later, in cooperation with the Highland View Hospital, Mrs. Behrens designed a number of other garments suitable for patients who had a limited range of motion or who used braces. Included in this group of garments were men's slacks, women's slacks, robes, slips, dresses, costs, and four garments for children.[5]

By the later part of 1963, seventeen garments had been designed and the first public showing was held at the national convention of the National Rehabilitation Association at Miami Beach, Florida. In January of the following year, the "Specially Designed Clothing Service" was made a separate department of the Vocational Guidance and Rehabilitation Services, with a group of clients employed to produce the clothing. A catalog was issued at that time featuring forty items of clothing, complete with a measuring chart and price list to facilitate mail orders.[5] In the current catalog, there are over forty items of clothing listed.

Men's wardrobes are usually less complicated than those of women, but men who are physically handicapped also have special needs. For those confined to wheelchairs, specially designed garments are made to measure by Leinenweber, Inc., of Chicago and available by mail order. The design adaptations, used by Leinenweber, were suggested earlier by the late Helen Cookman and by Muriel Zimmerman (of the Institute of Physical Medicine and Rehabilitation, New York University Medical Center), and also by Clarice Scott (then Clothing Specialist in the Agricultural Research Service of the U.S. Department of Agriculture). Featured in the designs used by Leinenweber are a short front rise and longer back rise in trousers, shorter suit jacket, jacket vents long enough to accommodate body braces, coats with shortened backs, and zippers inserted in trousers legs to accommodate leg braces and to facilitate toileting.[5]

One of the most important objectives in providing specially designed clothing for the physically handicapped is to make dressing and undressing easier. Many articles have appeared in the rehabilitation literature, beginning in the early 1940s when occupational therapists concerned themselves with the dressing problems of cerebral palsied children. Later publications have dealt with the use of devices of various kinds of aid in dressing and grooming for both children and adults.

The interest of home economists in serving some of the needs of the physically handicapped was expressed in the interdisciplinary workshop on "Rehabilitation of the Physically Handicapped in Homemaking Activities," conducted at Highland Park, Illinois, in 1963 (sponsored by the American Home Economics Association and the Rehabilitation Services Administration, Social and Rehabilitation Services, U.S. Department of Health, Education and Welfare). Proceedings of the workshop were recorded in a report released following the workshop. In 1969, a second interdisciplinary workshop was conducted (under a grant from the Rehabilitation Services Administration, Social and Rehabilitation Service, U.S. Department of Health, Education and Welfare) to evaluate past programs and to plan for the future. The major objectives were to explore the role of home economists as members of rehabilitation teams in restoring the handicapped to productive family and community life and to define the need for research and education programs.

A federal government program, concerned directly with the physically handicapped, is the President's Committee on the Employment of the Handicapped. While this committee itself is not concerned directly with clothing, a sub-committee, the Women's Committee, is concerned with clothing, and at the 1966 national annual meeting, the Women's Committee provided a program feature on clothing for the physically handicapped. Also, in 1966, the Vocational Guidance and Rehabilitation Services of Cleveland, Ohio, conducted a national seminar on "Functionally Designed Clothing and Aids for the Chronically Ill and Disabled," which was supported in part by a Rehabilitation Services Administration training grant, Social and Rehabilitation Service, U.S. Department of Health, Education and Welfare. The purpose of the seminar was to bring together a highly selected group of thirty-two people representing many disciplines to discuss all aspects and problems concerned with special clothing needs, and to create better understanding among the many disciplines concerned.[8]

An outstanding addition to the literature was the book, *Homemaking for the Handicapped* (by Elizabeth Eckhardt May, Eleanor M. Boettke, and Neva R. Waggoner, 1966) which included three chapters on clothing. The second edition of the book was published in 1974 under title of *Independent Living for the Handicapped and the Elderly.* In 1977, four bibliographies were published on rehabilitation of the handicapped which included clothing for both the handicapped and the elderly. These bibliographies are listed in the Appendix.

The first national conference devoted to "Clothing for People with Special Needs" was held in January, 1977 at the University of Alabama under the direction of Mary Catherine

Beasley, Director, and members of her staff in Continuing Education in Home Economics, Division of Continuing Education. The primary purpose of the clothing conference was to bring together an interdisciplinary group of persons who were concerned with various aspects of the clothing needs of persons with physical limitations. The conference program provided an opportunity to explore the physical, psychological, and social aspects of selecting, adapting, and designing clothing for the handicapped and the aging, and to gain understanding of motor function, body abnormalities, and sensory deficiences in relation to clothing. Attendance at the conference was 166, representing twenty-nine states and the District of Columbia in addition to Alabama.

In the fall of 1976, initial work was done by the College of Home Economics at the Virginia Polytechnic Institute and State University, with the support of the Cooperative State Research Service, to access and project research needs in home economics in an attempt to provide a basis for evaluation of current research and for the projection of future research in home economics. A number of people were asked to write position statements concerning conditions as they now exist, problems in society, and projections for the future, and to identify researchable problems existing within specific subject matter areas. In the spring of 1977, a workshop on "Home Economics Research Assessment, Planning and Projection" (sponsored by the Agricultural Research Policy Advisory Committee and the Association of Administrators of Home Economics) was held in Washington, D.C., at which the situation papers and suggested research projects were reviewed and revised in order to finally determine values and priorities. Among the areas of textiles and clothing which were given consideration was that of special clothing needs.

Some sources of clothing for those with special needs were short-lived, but in the 1970s, a few more persons who were concerned with providing clothing for those with special needs, went into the business and have issued catalogs. A list appears in the Appendix.

CLOTHING FOR THE AGED

The earliest concerted activity in the field of aging by home economists was the national workshop on aging, conducted by the American Home Economics Association at Purdue University in 1962, at which clothing was one of the areas of consideration. The first book that devoted very much space to clothing for the aged was *Family Clothing* (by Mildred Thurow Tate and Oris Glisson, of the Virginia Polytechnic Institute, published in 1961). The chapter on "The later years" was based on the research of the authors and selected literature from the field of gerontology. In 1966, chapters on clothing for the aged appeared in a number of books. *Clothing: A Study in Human Behavior* (by Mary Shaw Ryan, of Cornell University) included a chapter entitled "Psychological implications of clothing for the elderly," in which early research was cited. In *Homemaking for the Handicapped* and *Independent Living for the Handicapped and the Elderly,* the chapters on clothing included the elderly in addition to the handicapped.

Beginning in the late 1950s and continuing into the 1970s, graduate students at a number of universities did research on clothing needs, problems, attitudes, and preferences of older people and a contribution to this research was the bibliographies compiled at the University of Iowa by faculty of the Department of Home Economics. In 1962, Iva M. Bader compiled a comprehensive bibliography entitled "The Social Science Aspects of Clothing with Implications for Older Women," and two years later, Adeline M. Hoffman and Iva M. Bader compiled an annotated bibliography entitled "Social Science Aspects of Clothing for Older Women," in which they brought together, in a more useful form, publications on the subject up to that time. In 1977, the second edition of the annotated bibliography was published, and in 1975, an annotated bibliography on clothing for the elderly, compiled by Audrey Newton, Barbara Ann Nelson and Dorcas Odu, was published at the University of Nebraska.

The Institute of Gerontology at the University of Iowa offered short courses on aging for nursing and retirement home administrators; on the program of one of the short courses, Adeline Hoffman spoke on the "social and therapeutic value of clothing" for nursing home and retirement home residents, and later contributed a chapter entitled "Clothing: Social and Therapeutic Values" for the book, *Nursing and Retirement Home Administration,* published in 1966. Increasing interest of home economists in the area of clothing for the aged was evidenced by the continual requests for copies of bibliographies and other publications, and it was this evidence of interest that led to the publication of the book in 1970, edited and compiled by Adeline M. Hoffman, entitled *The Daily Needs and Interests of Older People,* which included a chapter on clothing.

Some of the early literature of the Gerontological Society made brief mention of clothing, but it was not until 1968 that much space was given to clothing. In that year, a chapter on clothing, by Iva M. Bader, appeared in *Working with Older People — A Guide to Practice,* Volume IV, The Aging Person: Needs and Practices (published by the Gerontological Society); two years later, the Public Health Service, U.S. Department of Health, Education and Welfare, used a shorter version of the chapter in one of its own publications. In the 1970s, articles on clothing by home economists have appeared in *The Gerontologist,* a publication of the Gerontological Society.

Interest in the field of clothing for the physically handicapped and the aged is reflected in the increasing number of conferences, workshops, and seminars conducted by home economists, often with guest speakers from related disciplines; in the number of articles which continue to appear in home economics and health-related publications; in the many bulletins on the subject which are issued by the Extension Service in many states, and the special training given to Extension Service personnel by Clothing Specialists. Also, courses in gerontology and in rehabilitation are being offered by home economists, which include consideration of special clothing needs, and some home economics faculty members at the colleges and universities are including "special clothing needs" in their courses in clothing selection, construction, and design.

REFERENCES

1. Brown, Mary Eleanor: Personal communication, December 10, 1974.
2. For the Handicapped — Clothes have Therapeutic Value, *New York Herald Tribune*, August 15, 1958.
3. Rusk, Howard A. and Taylor, Eugene J.: *Living With a Disability*. New York, Blakiston, 1953.
4. Fact sheet on Helen Cookman, New York University, Office of Information Service, October 21, 1958.
5. Hallenbeck, Phyllis N.: Special clothing for the handicapped — review of research and resources. *Rehabilitation Literature* 27(2):34-40, February, 1966.
6. Tharp, Bernice J.: *The Handicapped — Clothing Implication*. Clothing News and Research Findings. University Park, Pa, Cooperative Extension Service, Pennsylvania State U, 1964.
7. Odell, Van Davis: Personal communication, November 6, 1972.
8. *Functionally Designed Clothing and Aids for Chronically Ill and Disabled*, Seminar Report, Vocational Guidance and Rehabilitation Services, Cleveland, Ohio, 1966.

Chapter 4

PSYCHOLOGICAL ASPECTS OF CLOTHING

PEOPLE of all ages and in all circumstances of life are aware of the importance of appearance in perception of self and in their relations with other people. Desire for approval is always present, and "from the cradle to the grave, we clamor for our neighbor's attention" and for approval which gives us a feeling of well-being and self-confidence. Lawrence Langner, in *The Importance of Wearing Clothes*, states that "one of the greatest spiritual needs of people is the admiration of their fellow men and women, and here clothing plays a major role."[1]

Such expressions of the significance of clothing are found over and over again in the literature and in the experience of people. A woman who was hospitalized said she did not want any visitors as long as she had to wear a hospital gown, and when she was allowed to wear her own pretty nightgowns and bed jackets, she lifted the ban on visitors. Another woman, who had come to live in a retirement residence, immediately informed her grandson of her need for better clothes in order to properly relate to the other residents. Clothing has always been a kind of status symbol and expression of the individual personality. In the Shakespearian plays, there are numerous references to clothing, the most familiar of which is probably the one from Hamlet in which Polonious says, "Costly as thy purse can buy, but not expressed in fancy, rich, not gaudy, for apparel oft proclaims the man." In commenting on clothing as an expression of personality, George Dearborn, an early twentieth century psychologist said, "We might consider clothes as a vicarious second skin, almost an extension of the individual boundry, involving important relationships between the person and his environment, spiritual as well as material."[2]

AESTHETIC VALUE OF ATTRACTIVE CLOTHING

In the words of a philosopher of art, "the function of beauty is to lift the human spirit." Just as all people respond to the aesthetic stimulation of a beautiful sunset, a flower, or a work of art, so do they respond to the aesthetic stimulation of attractive clothing. The elements of attractiveness in clothing are color, texture, design, decoration accented with such accessories as jewelry, and distinctiveness and individuality. For those whose environment is limited by age, conditions of health, or physical handicaps, attractive clothing can provide aesthetic stimulation and can also lift the spirit and enhance the sense of personal worth. Beauty provides feelings of serenity, well-being and happiness, and lessens feelings of tension, anger, hostility, and depression. Response to beauty can be a shared experience as when members of a group dress up for a social event. Such shared experiences, in which each person makes a contribution by a degree of dressing up, tend to bannish feelings of boredom and loneliness, for beauty stimulates not only one's aesthetic sensitivity, but also one's imagination.

The clothing of each individual becomes a part of the environment in which the person is present, and thus contributes, in a sense, to the environment of all others present, just as a plant, a flower, or a picture becomes a part of the environment of all who are present. Beauty is a need, not something extra that might or might not be provided. People seek beauty in their homes, their gardens, their travels, in their churches, their public buildings and places of meeting, and in their total environment.

PHYSICALLY HANDICAPPED ADULTS

Physical handicaps that are readily visible make the need for attractive clothing much more important, so that the observer sees not primarily a physically handicapped person, but rather an attractively dressed person who also has a physical handicap. Attractive clothing has the same effect on the physically handicapped person, that of feeling like a well-dressed person who also has a physical handicap. As more physically handicapped people take their places in occupational life and community life, they will be recognized as people rather than as objects of pity or curiosity, and attractive clothing will enhance their public image.

Clothing is generally recognized as one of the status symbols for all people and by all people, and for those whose status has been affected by a physical handicap, attractive clothing takes on great importance. According to Wright, "there is a tendency, where characteristics conveying status implications are concerned, for inferiority of one kind to spread to the total inferiority of the person."[3] Thus, the single physical handicaps that are visible often lead observers to conclude that the person is totally handicapped and therefore of little worth. This is one of the cruelist results of visible handicaps and is often referred to as an attitudinal barrier which can become a greater obstacle than a physical barrier for physically handicapped persons. Attitudes of people, in all conditions of life, are based largely on first impressions, and clothing plays a major role in first impressions. As Will Rogers once said, "We don't get a second chance to make a first impression." Attractive clothing tends to accentuate favorable features and minimize limitations, and also leads the observer to a greater understanding and appreciation of the potential of physically handicapped persons.

Among the most seriously handicapped are those with amputations and spinal cord injuries. In discussing the psychological implications of amputations, Garrett says —

> the word *cosmesis*, which pertains to adornment, beautification or decoration, is widely used in the field of prosthesis restoration as a synonym for problems associated with one's visible appearance. The cosmetic effect is greater for the upper extremity amputees of both sexes and for female lower extremity amputees, since in both instances, the extremity is not normally covered by clothing. Because of our mode of dress, it is a lesser problem for male lower extremity amputees and for young children whose state of psychosexual development makes for less concern over matters of personal appearance. With the advent of adolescence, this situation changes

dramatically and cosmetic considerations become of urgent importance.[4]

In further discussion of psychological implications of amputations, Bonner explains that "the loss of a lower extremity is a very traumatic experience and most patients go into a fairly marked depression following the surgery because they view themselves as having a distorted body. Their apprehensions of losing physical ability, work ability and self-esteem may become major problems in their rehabilitation process."[5] For such patients, attractive and appropriate clothing helps in regaining their self-esteem.

Spinal cord injuries create many problems that stem from disabilities. In writing on the total adjustment of paraplegics, Cogswell declares that

> all paraplegics face problems which evolve from the stigma of disability. In the hospital, medical personnel help paraplegics develop a self-image of independence and personal worth. Although difficulties are encountered, it is easier to establish and maintain this self-image in the sheltered social environment of the hospital than in the world outside. When paraplegics return to their homes and communities, definitions of their disability as a social stigma reach their height. In our society, the disabled role is socially devalued. Effective socialization results through learning to reduce the stigmatizing effects of disability. Physical disability, like most stigmas, is not equally stigmatizing in all social situations. It varies with the paraplegic's definition and projection of self as worthy or demeaned and with his skill in managing other's definitions of his disability. Uncertain of what the response of others will be, paraplegics tend to expect the worst. They are apprehensive that the attention of others may be focused on the disability and that other aspects of self will be treated as irrelevant.[6]

Though paraplegics are usually seen in wheelchairs, their image can be greatly improved by attractive clothing, proportioned and adapted to their special needs.

PHYSICALLY HANDICAPPED CHILDREN

In describing a pretty girl or a brave boy, clothing is always mentioned, for clothing is a part of the individual, at least a part of the body image. The social connotation of clothing is learned at an early age and is at a peak during adolescence. There is great importance attached to imitating peer image and wearing "what they are wearing" at the time.

Acceptance by their nonhandicapped peers is very important to physically handicapped children. They consider clothes that their nonhandicapped counterparts are wearing to be the right kind of clothes to own and to wear, and they dislike to deviate very much from the appearance of other children. According to a study by Cannon, physically handicapped children are more clothes conscious than nonhandicapped children. Clothes consciousness may be defined as heightened awareness of clothing and recognition of its social value. It includes awareness of one's own clothing, the clothing others wear, how the clothing worn affects the feelings of others and how clothing worn by others affects feelings toward them.[7]

All people, and especially children, tend to like people better who are well dressed and tend to treat them with greater respect. This is one of the reasons why children want new clothes to wear when school opens in the fall in anticipation of creating a favorable impression on their peers and even on their teachers, and it is also the reason why they want to wear clothes received as Christmas gifts as soon as school opens after the Christmas holidays.

Because of the narrower range of social activities of physically handicapped children, their wardrobes are usually smaller than those of nonhandicapped children. Although they have more problems in finding clothes that fit well and also satisfy their other needs, they generally prefer ready-made clothes adapted to their needs rather than clothes made for them at home that might look quite different from the clothes of other children. Whenever possible, children should have the opportunity for some choice in the purchasing of their clothing. Clothing choice is an expression of personality and independence and provides a different sense of ownership than does clothing chosen by others for physically handicapped children.

THE MENTALLY RETARDED

The meaning of clothing to mentally retarded persons and their reaction to clothing depends largely on their degree of retardation, their awareness of their environment, and their reaction to other people. Many mentally retarded persons respond to the aesthetic stimulation of color, design, decoration, and other forms of beauty in their environment, which are also present in clothing. They may or may not be aware of the reactions of other people to their clothing and the social significance of clothing in a theoretical sense, but many make some reaction to clothing in general. The mildly retarded respond to clothing and express interest in clothing in much the same way as their mentally normal counterparts, and for them, clothing serves the same personal and social needs.

In addition to the psychological effect of clothing on the mentally retarded individual, there is also the effect of the clothing of the mentally retarded person on the observer. One who first sees a well-dressed person and then learns that the person is mentally retarded is likely to place some value on the person rather than totally discarding the person as of no social value. Appearance has been called "nonverbal communication" because immediate reaction and social acceptance is based largely on appearance before any other factors concerning the individual are known.

Some research has been reported on the psychological effects of clothing on mentally ill patients in institutions, but little if any research has been reported on the psychological effects of clothing on the mentally retarded. One recent study of institutionalized persons who were either severely or profoundly mentally retarded indicated that there was some response to clothing even at these levels of retardation. The mentally retarded persons involved in the research responded to bright colors, newness, and style features such as large patch pockets on the front of the garments, with expressions of interest and excitement. However, their initial interest and excitement in response to the experimental garments was short-lived in comparison to mentally normal persons who have a longer attention span and whose awareness of new clothing lasts for a longer period of time.[8]

THE CHRONICALLY ILL

Some families are able to make provision in their homes for the care of older family members who are chronically ill, but most families are not able to make such provision, and the chronically ill take up residence in nursing homes or other care facilities. Though some chronically ill persons are bed ridden, the majority are not, and for them, clothing has important connotations. To be sure, there is little eventfulness in the lives of nursing home residents, but even the little there is can be highlighted through the effective use of clothing.

For those not bedridden the wearing of daytime clothing rather than night wear or lounging wear is very important. This creates a feeling of eventual recovery and return to normal health rather than prolonged convalescence or no hope of leaving the nursing home. In a nursing home situation, a bit of dressing up on occasion has its values. Even a change of clothing in the afternoon can make a social event out of a tea or other midafternoon refreshment, especially if there is a guest coming or a local group to entertain the residents. A bit of dressing up is always in order at holiday time to relive some of the joy of the season and to feel a sense of participation in what other people are experiencing at the same time. To create a personal sense of festivity, a symbol of the holiday can be used to adorn the dress or even the bed jacket, such as a tiny shamrock on St. Patrick's Day.

Most nursing home routine is beyond the control of the residents, but they might still gain a sense of personal control and achievement through choice of their clothing. Those who bring clothing items as gifts to family members or friends in nursing homes could enhance the value of gifts by making some provision for choice, even just choice of color. People in nursing homes have much less need for new clothing than those in normal health, living in their own homes. However, there is an important value in newness. It helps to create a feeling of anticipation, of looking ahead into the future rather than looking back into the past when old clothes were new. New clothing becomes a kind of link with the outside world even though the residents may not be able to go outside the nursing home. Some old people cling to their old clothes like old friends, yet others feel a childish delight in newness. The reaction of the individual is based largely on condition of health, mental alertness, and hope of recovery, but for most chronically ill people in nursing homes, new clothing has some values.[9]

OLDER PEOPLE

It is generally true that clothing is somewhat less significant in the lives of older people than younger people because of gradually decreasing social activity, but there are circumstances in the lives of many older people that make clothing almost as important as it was in their adolescence or early adulthood. When older people move from where they had lived for a long time, there is need to establish new social relationships, so it becomes important to present a good appearance. Older people who move into the homes of their children have the same need to establish new social relationships in the community and with their children's associates. In moving from their own homes to retirement residences, there is also the need to establish new social relationships, and appearance has much to do with getting acquainted and making new friends. "Birds of a feather flock together" even among older people living in retirement residences and retirement communities.

Some older people experience a considerable loss of social identity when their children grow up and leave the family home. This social identity may have been an important source of ego support, and without it, something must take its place. For many older people, attractive clothing can provide some of the lost ego support. In the termination of employment or the husband's employment, there is often a great loss of status and ego support and the need to make up for the loss. Not only is there loss of relationships with former colleagues but also the loss of skill-related identity. Attractive clothing can bolster the ego and enhance the self-image of those experiencing such a loss. Other circumstances of life which call for the establishment of new social relationships are the loss of spouse, friends, and contemporaries by people who live well past their eightieth birthdays. After suffering feelings of loss and loneliness, they also find that attractive clothing can be helpful in reestablishing themselves socially and in finding companionship.

The loss of physical attractiveness among older people is sometimes referred to as the "insults of aging," but in a more positive sense, it has been called "beauty changing rather than beauty departing." Attractive clothing cannot reverse the order of physical change nor delay the process, but it can add to good self-image and personal dignity. Closely related to clothing as a part of the total appearance and a source of ego support is hair care and grooming. Some older women who maintain an active social life and who seek to maintain the appearance of custom and good taste increase their beauty care and their patronage of beauty care facilities. For other older women, the reverse is true because of limited social life, problems of transportation, cost, and decreased physical energy.[10]

REFERENCES

1. Langner, Lawrence: *The Importance of Wearing Clothes.* New York, Hastings, 1959.
2. Dearborn, George Van Ness: The psychology of clothes. *Psychological Monographs, XXVI (112):*172, 1918.
3. Wright, Beatrice A.: *Physical Disability — A Psychological Approach.* New York, Har-Row, 1960.
4. Garrett, James F. and Levine, Edna S. (Eds.): *Psychological Practice with the Physically Disabled.* New York, Columbia U Pr, 1962.
5. Bonner, Charles D.: *Medical Care and Rehabilitation of the Aged and Chronically Ill,* 3rd ed. Boston, Little, 1974.
6. Cogswell, Betty E.: Self-socialization and readjustment of paraplegics in the community. *Journal of Rehabilitation, 34*(3):11-13, 35, May-June, 1968.
7. Cannon, Mary Louise: Relationship of Clothing and Social Activities of Physically Handicapped and Non-Handicapped Children of Junior

High School Age. Master's Thesis, Iowa City, U of Iowa, 1969.

8. Olson, Turdy Leskovac: Clothing for the Institutionalized Severely and Profoundly Mentally Retarded. Master's Thesis, Madison, U of Wis, 1973.

9. Hoffman, Adeline M.: Clothing: social and therapeutic values. In Jacobs, H. Lee and Morris, W. W. (Eds.): *Nursing and Retirement Home Administration.* Ames, Iowa State University Press, 1966.

10. Hoffman, Adeline M.: Clothing. In Hoffman, Adeline M. (Ed.): *The Daily Needs and Interests of Older People.* Springfield, Thomas, 1970.

Chapter 5

ANALYSIS IN SOLUTION
TO CLOTHING PROBLEMS

THE major factors with which all people are generally concerned in satisfying their clothing needs are color, design, fashion, fit, comfort, and cost. In addition to these factors, the physically handicapped also have the problem of ease in dressing and undressing, which is often the factor of greatest importance. Because of physical limitations, the process of dressing and undressing becomes a difficult and time-consuming task, and for some, it may be an impossible task. Most physically handicapped people want to become independent and self-sufficient in the activities of daily living, including dressing and undressing. Problems in dressing and undressing are also common among the elderly, the chronically ill, and the mentally retarded.

Instruction in dressing and undressing is given to patients in hospitals by nurses, occupational therapists, and physical therapists. Some respond to the instruction better than others, learning to cope with their problems and finally mastering the techniques of dressing and undressing, while others continue to need assistance after they have been discharged from hospitals and rehabilitation centers. It was this continuing need for assistance that brought about greater effort to design clothing to make dressing and undressing easier. When the process of dressing and undressing is very difficult, time-consuming, and frustrating, some physically handicapped and also chronically ill persons avoid the dressing process altogether by wearing night clothes in the daytime. Gaining complete independence in dressing and undressing requires continual effort; the use of manageable clothing plays an important part in the achievement of this goal.

The physical conditions that create problems in dressing and undressing may be classified as muscular weakness, joint limitations and limitations in range of motion and reach, partial or total lack of coordination, poor balance, spasticity, use of braces and prostheses, paralysis, deformities, amputations, and single handedness. In seeking solutions to clothing problems, it is necessary to know the nature of the physical disability rather than the cause. Understanding the technical terminology that relates to each physical condition is not necessary in order to analyze clothing problems and arrive at solutions. However, persons dealing with the problems, sooner or later, do become interested in the causes, and in order to satisfy their intellectual curiosity, they learn about the origins of handicapping conditions. For purposes of satisfying clothing needs, only the physical condition, the patients capabilities, and what can be expected in terms of improvement or deterioration must be known.

Clothing needs, to ease the problems in dressing and undressing and to increase efficiency in use, may be stated in general terms which apply to many physical conditions. There are other needs which apply to certain specific conditions. Those that apply to many physical conditions include (1) selection of fabric, (2) construction and location of openings to facilitate dressing and undressing, (3) number, type, and location of fastenings for ease in use, and (4) design of garments for comfort and ease of movement. In addition to needs concerned with dressing and undressing, clothing must be adapted in terms of fit and use and must provide for the psychological needs concerned with attractive appearance, especially among those who have readily visible handicaps such as amputations, deformities, and mobility problems that require the use of braces, crutches, and wheelchairs.

SELECTION OF FABRIC AND CONSTRUCTION PROCESSES TO MEET SPECIFIC NEEDS

The wide variety of fabrics available provides opportunity to select fabrics to meet specific needs. Fabrics for the clothing of those who have specific needs must be carefully selected in order to meet all the known needs rather than a single need.

Thus, it is necessary to know something of the daily activities of the individual, mobility limitations, and other physical conditions which relate to fabric characteristics.

Fabric Strength

One of the needs of many physically handicapped people is fabric strength to withstand strain and abrasion. Reaching and pulling causes strain on fabrics, and much reaching and pulling occurs in the daily activities of physically handicapped people, particularly those who have mobility problems. Pulling clothes on as many paraplegics must do, reaching for things at a distance, and grasping and reaching in operating wheelchairs and in using walkers are some of the daily activities that cause strain on fabrics. Abrasion is caused primarily by constant rubbing of clothing against prostheses, crutches, and braces particularly at joints such as knees. Fabrics of firm construction, high tensile strength, and smooth finish are most resistant to abrasion.

Reinforcements

To counteract abrasion, reinforcements are needed at points of greatest wear. These include knees, elbows, underarm areas, and other places on garments according to crutches, prostheses, and braces used. Reinforcements may be made of self-material, vinyl, leather, or other durable material such as industrial nylon. For underarm reinforcements, self-material is the best choice. At other places on garments, reinforcements may be made of contrasting colors and different textures in order to be decorative as well as practical. Most reinforcements are sewn to the outside of garments, both ready-made and garments made at home. On trousers for dress wear, reinforcements are sewn to the inside of the knee area or linings are attached to cover areas of greatest wear. In addition to reinforcements to counteract abrasion, other points of wear that need strengthening are the ends of inserted zippers, buttonholes, the ends of welt pockets, and the upper corners of patch pockets.

Seam Construction

Durability of garments as a whole may be enhanced by the kind of seams used. The strongest seams are those which are double stitched, such as fell and welt. In addition to the double stitching, seam edges in fell seams are enclosed so there is no possibility of fraying. Durability is also affected by the length of stitch used in seam construction, the shorter stitch being the more durable. Plain seams, which are used in kimono and raglan sleeve construction, should be reinforced. Seam edges of the underarm seams, which must be clipped in order to lay flat in the curved areas, reduces their ability to withstand strain.

Cleaning Methods

Frequent cleaning of garments is necessary, so all fabrics should be launderable rather than require dry cleaning. Labels on ready-made garments and on fabrics purchased to make garments at home give the necessary information on cleaning methods to be used and limitations of the fabric. Fastenings and trimmings on garments should be launderable to avoid the need to remove them for laundering, then sewing them on again after laundering. Fabrics should withstand high temperatures and strong washing compounds and bleaches used in institutional laundering. Only outer garments such as jackets and coats need not be launderable.

Soil repellent and stain resistant finishes are very important in fabrics used for garments to be worn by some physically handicapped people. Some have difficulty in eating and food that drops on their clothing may leave stains. Drooling is another source of soiling and staining when protective bibs are not used. In the daily activities of children, much time is spent in outdoor play which may involve crawling and sitting on playgrounds. This causes constant soiling of garments and the need for frequent laundering. Among both children and adults who have bowel and bladder control problems there is frequent staining of clothing with fecal matter and urine.

Comfort

Absorbency is one of the characteristics of natural fibers that contribute to comfort, and cotton is one of the most absorbent. This is why so many people prefer garments made of cotton fabrics, especially undergarments. The strength of cotton fabrics is increased by the use of tightly twisted yarns and tight weave, and strength is further increased when blended with synthetic fibers which are stronger but not as absorbent. Static electricity is characteristic of most synthetic fibers, particularly the polyesters, but this is reduced when blended with natural fibers. Static electricity causes garments to cling to the body instead of hanging freely. The clinging is especially difficult when it reveals braces and prostheses and affects mobility of crutch users and the appearance of those in wheelchairs. The ability to drape well rather than cling is necessary for comfort and good appearance and for efficient use of crutches and wheelchairs.

Excessive weight of fabrics creates discomfort for physically handicapped children and adults and also older people. Weight is burdensome, causes fatigue, and affects mobility. Instead of very heavy wool outergarments, fabrics of wool and synthetic fiber blends are lighter weight and more durable. To reduce weight and still provide warmth, coats may be lined with metallic-backed lining fabric which does away with the need for interlining. This is lighter weight than regular lining fabric plus interlining and provides the needed warmth.

Stretch and Texture

Stretch fabrics are particularly advantageous, as they withstand the various reaching motions that are hard on clothing. Knit fabrics and stretch woven fabrics have the advantage of stretch without strain and return to their original shape and dimensions. When using nonstretch fabrics, a part of a garment may be cut on the bias to provide stretch in a particular direction. Fabric textures have advantages and disadvantages.

Slippery textures are useful for those who must slide on and off upholstered seating and in and out of cars; for those who have to be picked up and carried, there might be danger of losing one's grip, resulting in a falling accident. Coarse textures would make handling easier and surer. Harsh textures, such as worsteds, can stand hard wear, but for many people they are uncomfortable, particularly older people with skin that is thin, dry, and sensitive. For older people, very soft textures are more appropriate. Napped or brushed textures in both knitted and woven fabrics are generally more comfortable than other textures and are a bit warmer and provide a smooth pleasant feeling.

Light Penetration

Opaqueness and transparency of fabrics should be considered for clothing worn over braces and prostheses. Garments made of opaque fabrics are best for those worn over braces and prostheses, particularly body braces above the waist and upper extremity prostheses. For those who have lower extremity prostheses and who wear body braces below the waist, shirts, blouses, and tops to be worn with slacks could be made of sheer transparent fabrics.

Cost Control

In achieving maximum wear of clothing to reduce total clothing cost, "all season" fabrics may be selected so that clothing may be worn the year round instead of for only one season. An assortment of attractive colors and color combinations, textures, prints, and woven stripes and plaids provide aesthetic interest and practical values and could keep a year-round wardrobe from becoming monotonous.

FASTENINGS FOR GARMENTS

One of the greatest difficulties in the process of dressing and undressing is the reaching and manipulation of fastenings of many kinds at many places on garments. Muscular weakness, loss of finger dexterity and eye-hand coordination, and limited range of reach and motion are the main factors that affect ability to handle fastenings. One of the simplest solutions to the problem of handling fastenings is to use garments that have no fastenings at all that require any manipulation. These include dresses, skirts, trousers, and slacks that have elasticized waistlines, and sweaters and blouses that slip on over the head and have no fastenings. All garments cannot be adapted to such simple design, but in general, the fewer fastenings used, the less difficult the problem becomes. Also the fewest kinds of fastenings used lessens the problem, especially for those who have learning limitations.

Buttons and Other Small Fasteners

Small buttons, hooks and eyes, snap fasteners, and prong buckles are among the most difficult types of fastenings to handle. All of them require firm grasp, finger dexterity, and good eye-hand coordination. Large buttons, at least the size of a nickel, are easier to grasp and can be used by some people with hand limitations. Buttons sewn on garments with long shanks or with elastic thread ease the grasping of the buttons and the process of buttoning. Also, large metal hooks and bars, which are used as a single fastening at the top of openings in men's

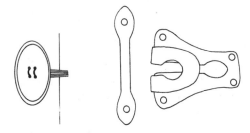

Figure 1. Button sewn to a garment with a long thread shank for ease in grasping and fastening, and large metal hook and bar.

trousers, can be used on garments for those with hand limitations. Magnetic fasteners, which are relatively easy to handle, nylon plastic clasps called Bonnie Clasps®, and other types of fasteners that require little manipulation are found in catalogs of special devices for the physically handicapped and also at the notion goods counters in fabric departments of many stores. For children who need practice in handling buttons, ties, and other fasteners on their own clothing, such fasteners can be put on the outer garments of their large dolls and teddy bears.

Zippers

The two most important types of fasteners that facilitate the process of dressing and undressing and lessen the physical effort, time, and frustration involved are zippers and Velcro®. Both zippers and Velcro can be used to replace other kinds of fasteners. Zippers, also called slide fasteners, may be inserted in any opening in a garment at any location. To avoid the difficulty of grasping the small zipper pull at the top of a zipper, a ring about the size of a quarter may be attached, which is easier to grasp. Decorative zipper pulls may also be used, made of materials of various kinds in sizes large enough to grasp easily in closing and opening zippers.

The origin of zippers dates back to 1892, when Whitcomb L. Judson designed a metal chain of hooks and eyes which he laced into his shoes before putting them on. The chain had a sliding cam which could be pulled with a string that caused the hooks and eyes to fit together. Fourteen years later, interlocking hooks were attached to a cloth tape for use in clothing, but the name "zipper" did not come into use until 1925 when these fasteners were applied to galoshes and later to luggage. Two years later, zippers were applied to clothing. The first zippers were made of metal and it was in the late 1950s that nylon zippers came into use.[1]

Velcro

Velcro, which is also called pressure tape, is a form of fastener composed of two layers of tape, one layer with fine nylon fiber hooks and the other with fine nylon fiber loops, which interlock with a small amount of pressure and may be separated with a small amount of pulling. This type of fastener may be used anywhere on a garment and is often used in openings in trousers, slacks, skirts, and dresses, and also on undergarments. Velcro is available in various forms and the most useful is linear form in three-quarter inch and one inch widths. Other forms are small circles and squares for specific uses. The first Velcro was made in white only but is now available in many colors.

 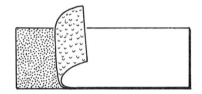

Figure 2. Velcro® in block and linear form.

Figure 3. Use of Velcro blocks to substitute for buttons and buttonholes to give a garment a buttoned appearance.

To give a garment the appearance of being buttoned, buttons are removed and sewn on over the buttonholes. Then small squares or circles of Velcro are sewn on where the buttons were removed and on back of the buttonholes. The garment is fastened by pressing the two Velcro surfaces together. In placing Velcro pieces to facilitate closures where buttons have been sewn over buttonholes, it is important to place Velcro pieces so they coordinate to form a smooth, accurate closing for the garment. The hook side of the Velcro tape should be away from the body and the loop side on the garment surface closest to the body. When the garment is laundered, the Velcro pieces should be closed to prevent an accumulation of lint on the Velcro surfaces which would render them less effective in future use.

The inspiration for the development of Velcro came from burdock burrs that stuck to clothing in walking through a field. When this happened to Swiss engineer George de Mestral, he wondered how this could happen, so he looked at the burrs under a magnifying glass and found that a burr was a collection of tiny hooks. When the hooks touched clothing, they dug into the fabric and it took some pulling apart to separate them. From his experience with burrs, the Swiss engineer discovered a totally new way of fastening things; after much experimenting, he developed a combination of hooks and loops that locked together. The name Velcro is derived from the first syllable of velvet and from the French word *crochet*, a small hook. First introduced in the early 1950s, Velcro was adapted by the airlines for attaching seat covers and seat back covers, by doctors in taking blood pressure, and by decorators for many purposes when it became available in the United States.[1]

Since its introduction in the United States, Velcro has been used extensively for closures in a variety of garments for the physically handicapped. Belts with buckles may be difficult to handle by those with hand limitations and such buckles may be replaced with Velcro. Buckles on shoes may also be replaced with Velcro, and zippers may replace laces in shoes. Such changes on shoes can be made by orthopedic shoemakers or

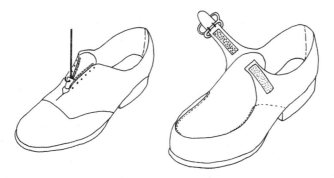

Figure 4. Velcro used to replace buckle closure on shoes and zipper used to replace laces. Top part of buckle may be sewn to strap to give appearance of buckle closure. Zipper may be closed by inserting a long handled hook in zipper tab.

other shoemakers if adequate explanation of the needed changes are given and the Velcro and zippers are provided.

DESIGN, LOCATION, AND CONSTRUCTION OF OPENINGS

Center front openings are best for people who have limited reach and range of motion. Center back openings are even difficult for people without such limitations and for those with limitations, they may be not only difficult but impossible. Front openings should not be started so high that the uppermost fastening cannot be seen and must be felt to be located in the process of opening and closing. For those who are unable to take care of themselves and have problems of incontinence, back openings in garments may be more convenient for persons giving assistance. Whenever assistance is required in dressing and undressing, the time required is of utmost importance, so location of openings and type of fasteners used must be considered in terms of those that involve the least time of the person who assists in the dressing and undressing process.

Garment Openings

Garments, such as dresses and nightgowns with short front openings, that must be put on over the head cannot be used by those who cannot raise their arms above their heads. In their garments, the front openings must be extended downward in order to step into the garments. For slips, a long front opening must be provided, using Velcro or a zipper closure. Openings that are easy to reach and to manage reduce the time and stress involved in dressing and undressing. For those with a nonfunctional hand and arm, openings must be located so they will be easily accessible to the useful hand and arm with fastenings appropriate to the needs of the individual.

Figure 5. Velcro fastening on wrap-style dress with optional tie belt, and wrap-style skirt with Velcro fastening at the waistline.

A type of opening that requires the least physical exertion is the wrap style, which can be used for a number of outer garments and some undergarments. Wrap-style dresses may be fastened with Velcro and may open in the center front or wrap to the right or left of the center front to provide an interesting line. Skirts in wrap style may be A-line, gored, gathered, or pleated and, in addition to Velcro, they may be fastened with large buttons, trouser hooks, or ties. Skirts may be moved around the waistline so that the opening is at the side front, side back, or at any convenient location on the waistline. Wrap slips may also be made, providing enough lap and fastenings to hold them in the normal position on the wearer. Garments which can be opened flat and wrapped around a handicapped child take less time for the helper when a child cannot help in

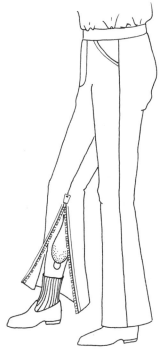

Figure 6. Opening in lower inseam of trousers with zipper closure to provide access to catheter equipment and urinal bag.

the dressing process. For those who cannot reach back openings in bras, front opening bras are available at many stores, from mail order catalogs, and from sources of special clothing. Bras that open in the back can be converted to front opening and can be fastened with Velcro, zippers, or hooks and eyes.

Trousers for men who wear leg braces and are confined to wheelchairs need side openings in addition to the fly to make it easier to get trousers on over braces, to provide access to catheter equipment and urinal bags, and for ease in toileting. As

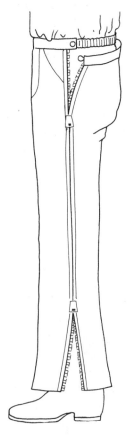

Figure 7. Two-way separating zipper in side seam of trousers for ease in covering long leg braces. Inner belt in trousers provides for dropping front or back to seat level for toileting.

suggested some years ago by the late Helen Cookman in collaboration with Muriel Zimmerman, inserting two-way separating zippers in the side seams of trousers from top to bottom makes provision for such needs. To hold trousers in place on the body during toileting, an inner belt can be added to trousers which buttons to the inside of the trousers in front or in back of the side seams, so that either the front or the back of the trousers can be dropped to seat level. If full length zippers are not needed, shorter zippers can be used to facilitate toileting.[2]

Necklines

The use of expandable necklines is one way of avoiding the need for fastening in garments such as shirts, blouses, sweaters, dresses, nightgowns, and pajama tops. These are especially adapted to people who have difficulty in managing fastenings but are able to grasp garments and raise their arms above their heads in the process of dressing and undressing. T-shirt-type neck openings and wider openings edged with rib knit fabric, which appear on sport shirts, are two common types of expandable neckline openings. Among the necklines finished with inside facings of self material, round necklines are less likely to tear in laundering than square or *V*-shaped necklines.

Peasant-type blouses for girls and women, with low elasticized necklines or drawstring necklines, are very easy to put on and take off over the head. Other types of expandable necklines that avoid fastenings and that can be put on and taken off over the head are necklines with low rolling collars, boat necklines, and short front openings either lapped or finished with a single facing.

Sleeves

Openings at the ends of sleeves, without fastenings, facilitate dressing and undressing. In garments for handicapped children who cannot dress themselves, long sleeves should be wide enough at the ends so that a person dressing children can reach up the sleeves and pull the hands through. Semifitted long sleeves can be wide enough to get the hands through without fastenings of any kind. Long sleeves on men's shirts usually have cuffs that either button or are fastened with cuff links. To avoid buttoning and unbuttoning and manipulating cuff links, buttons can be sewed on with elastic thread so the buttoned cuff expands enough to let the hand through in dressing and to pull the hand out in undressing. Cuff links, which are joined by a small metal link, can be adapted by discarding the link and substituting elastic thread to allow the cuffs to open enough to let the hand pass through in dressing and to withdraw the hand in undressing. Also, cuff links may be made by joining two buttons together with elastic thread and can be used in the same way as cuff links joined with elastic thread. For those with paralysis or malformation in an upper limb, which causes difficulty in dressing, zippers can be inserted in the sleeve seams and side seams of shirts, blouses, and jackets. In full length coats and dresses, the side seam zippers need to be only long enough for ease in dressing.

In peasant blouses with long, full sleeves, elastic can be inserted in a narrow casing or a narrow hem at the ends of the sleeves instead of cuffs or sleeve bands that would need fastenings of some kind. If sleeves are cut longer, sleeve ends could be elasticized by sewing very narrow elastic to the inside of the sleeves about one and one-half inches above the sleeve ends, and the ends of the sleeves then finished with a very narrow hem. The sleeve ends would then appear as narrow ruffles beyond the elastic. In a garment for a person with a completely paralyzed arm, which is difficult to insert into a sleeve, the sleeve seam can be completely opened and either Velcro or a zipper can be inserted in the seam so that the sleeves can be closed after the nonfunctional arm has been put in position through the armhole. In some cases, the upper section of the side seam may also be opened for greater ease in getting the arm into the armhole, and Velcro or a zipper closure may be used.

DESIGN FOR COMFORT AND EASE OF MOTION

Comfort is a necessity for all clothing. Regardless of the

other desirable features that may be present, clothing will not be worn if it is not comfortable. Many physically handicapped, elderly, and chronically ill people spend much of their time during the day in a sitting position, so their clothes must be comfortable in both a standing and sitting position. Dresses and skirts should be full enough so that there is no tightness in the abdominal and hip areas in a sitting position, and so that dresses and skirts do not ride up and expose the knees. Trousers and slacks for men must have enough ease for comfort in a sitting position and for the use of side front pockets. Also in a sitting position, high collars on women's dresses, blouses, and sweaters tend to ride up and are uncomfortable and unattractive, so for women who spend much of their time in a sitting position, another neckline finish would be a better choice. Inside facings are useful as neckline finishes on many types of garments and should be sewn down to avoid bunching up or turning to the outside of the garment. Turning neckline facings back to the inside of garments could involve painful reaching.

Garments for all people with special needs should be the right size so that garments fit well and are not too tight or too bulky. Elastic at the waistlines of dresses, blouses, and slacks should have easy stretch rather than limited stretch in order to not be so restrictive as to cause discomfort. Those who purchase the garments should be sure of the size needed and know specific measurements in certain dimension, such as length from waistline to crotch for trousers and slacks. Garments that fit well must also facilitate ease of motion and accommodate to the need for covering braces and prostheses.

For those with limited range of arm motion, raglan sleeves make dressing and undressing easier than set-in sleeves. Armholes in raglan sleeves are usually cut deeper which makes reaching into the sleeves easier in the process of dressing; also, there is greater ease across the shoulders which makes reaching easier. In children's clothing, raglan sleeves adapt to growth of children, whereas garments with set-in sleeves appear to be outgrown much sooner.

Ease of motion is generally facilitated through the use of knit fabrics and stretch woven fabrics, and for greater ease across the shoulder area in garments that have set-in sleeves, action pleats may be added below a narrow back yoke. The pleats should be located close to the armseye lines instead of in the center of the back in order to provide the greatest ease where it is needed. To facilitate arm motion, especially upward, gussets may be inserted in the underarm sleeve seam of set-in sleeves or in the curve of raglan or kimono type sleeves. Diamond-shaped gussets can provide enough ease so there is no splitting of under arm seams when much reaching must be done.

EFFECT OF ASSISTIVE DEVICES
ON CLOTHING NEEDS

The use of prostheses, braces, crutches, and wheelchairs bring about certain clothing needs which are relatively easy to

Figure 8. Turtle neck style in blouses, dresses, sweaters, and sport shirts to cover the tops of Milwaukee braces, and stand-up ruffles above the neckline in girl's blouses and dresses.

satisfy. Clothing worn over prostheses should be made of opaque fabric to disguise the prostheses. For those prostheses which have a joint that must be oiled to work smoothly, there is danger of oil stains appearing on clothing worn over the prostheses. Such clothing should always be washable rather than require dry cleaning. The attachment of some prostheses takes more room than the original appendage, so there must be allowance made in clothing to fit over the prostheses in order to be comfortable and avoid excessive abrasion.

Braces

Garments worn over braces should have adequate allowance for the braces to avoid constant abrasion. Milwaukee braces, which reach up to the base of the head in back and under the

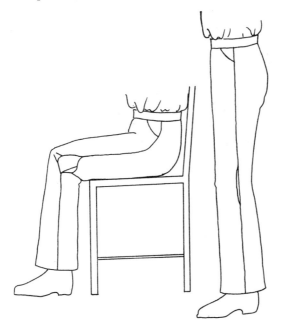

Figure 9. Inserted pleat at knee in side seam of trousers to provide ease and avoid excessive abrasion from the knee joint of braces.

chin in front, create a problem of clothing design to cover the tops of the braces. One solution is the use of turtle necklines, wide enough at the base to accommodate the braces, with a high enough section above the neckline to reach to the top of the braces. Doubleknit fabric or sweaterknit fabric adapt well to this need. Another way of covering the tops of Milwaukee braces in garments for girls is by adding a stand-up ruffle above the neckline, either elasticized at the neckline or gathered with a drawstring in a casing at the neckline. This would require alteration of a pattern to provide the extra length and fullness in the neckline area.

To avoid excessive wear on clothing, all surfaces of braces should be as smooth as possible, and at joints, reinforcement patches can be sewn to the inside of garments. Among the strongest fabrics for reinforcement patches is industrial nylon. Iron-on reinforcement patches can be used on the outside of garments, and parts of garments where there is greatest wear can be lined. To avoid excessive wear at the knees of trousers and slacks for those who wear long leg braces, a pleat can be inserted in the side seam or inseam at the knee area, similar to pockets in the side seams of dresses and skirts. In a standing position, the inserted pleats do not show. For help in pulling on trousers and slacks over long leg braces, zippers or Velcro can be inserted in the side seams or inseams far enough up the legs to provide the needed ease.

Crutches

One of the major clothing needs of crutch users is reinforcements where crutches rub against clothing, especially in the underarm area and sleeves when crutches that encircle the arms are used. The underarm seams of raglan or kimono sleeves should be reinforced, and gussets may be inserted in the underarm seams of both set-in and raglan sleeves to provide for greater ease of movement. The sleeves of coats should not be wide and bulky for those who use elbow crutches (that grip the arm just below the elbow).

With the use of crutches, there is a tendency for garments to

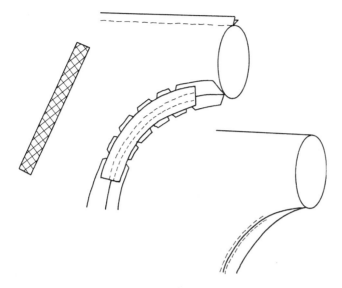

Figure 10. Reinforcement of underarm seams of raglan and kimono sleeves with self-fabric cut on the bias or other matching fabric or seam binding.

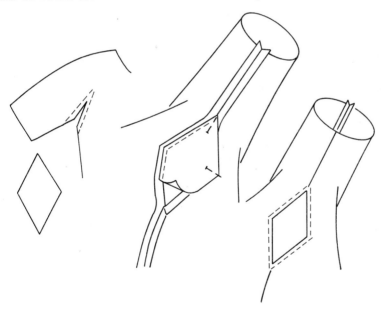

Figure 11. One-piece gusset inserted in underarm seam to provide for greater ease of movement.

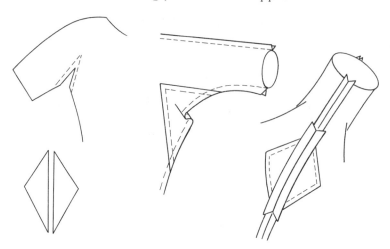

Figure 12. Two-piece gusset inserted in underarm seam to provide for greater ease of movement.

lift up from the normal position on the body. To reduce the lifting effect of crutch use, armholes should be cut high in garments such as dresses, blouses, shirts, jackets, and coats. Shirts and blouses and the tops of two piece dresses should be worn over the trousers, slacks, and skirts instead of tucked in to eliminate the appearance of garments being lifted out of position. In using crutches, there is also a tendency for sleeves to pull up, so long sleeves should be wide enough at the wrists to allow for upward movement. Long sleeves which are fitted at the wrist may be shortened for greater comfort. The motion involved in using crutches also requires ease across the back of the garment to avoid strain on armseye seams in set-in sleeves. Very full skirts and dresses may get in the way of crutches, so fullness should be limited to only the needs for comfort in a standing and sitting position and easy mobility.

Pockets in outer garments for those who use crutches should be closed with buttons, zippers, or Velcro in order to not lose the contents when hands are engaged with crutches. For greater safety, pockets can be attached to the inside of outer garments using the same types of closures.

Wheelchairs

The use of wheelchairs as a means of mobility brings about many clothing needs, and those who must use wheelchairs usually have more numerous and more severe impairments than those who can move about with the aid of crutches or canes. In most cases, there is some paralysis, which is the most limiting factor. The majority of wheelchair users are quadriplegics, paraplegics, hemiplegics or victims of stroke, amputees, and those who suffer from conditions such as muscular dystrophy and multiple sclerosis.

Figure 13. Narrow yoke and action pleats close to shoulders to provide ease across the back of the garment.

Knit fabrics and woven stretch fabrics adapt well to the needs for comfort and freedom of movement; in addition to the amount of stretch in the fabrics, extra width is needed across the shoulders and chest for ease in maneuvering the chair. One way to get the extra width is through inverted pleats in the shoulder area where most of the ease is needed. Using a narrow back yoke, pleats may be added to the lower back bodice, locating the pleats close to the armseyes rather than at the center of the back or distributing the extra fullness across the entire back. In addition to the fullness across the back and chest areas, sleeves should have extra width and should not be tightly tapered at the wrists, in order to avoid binding during the movement of the chair. Constant rubbing of the sleeves on the arms of the chair as the chair is propelled causes some wear, which can be avoided by the use of protective sleeve guards that fit over the arms.

Figure 14. Sleeve guard for wheelchair users to protect sleeves from excessive wear in propelling wheelchairs.

Pockets

Pockets should be located where they can be most easily

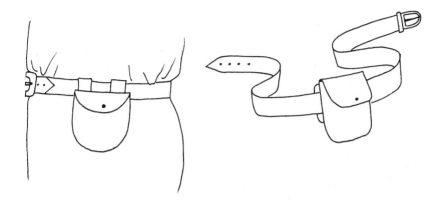

Figure 15. Pockets, attached to a waistline belt, which can be moved to the most convenient location for the wearer.

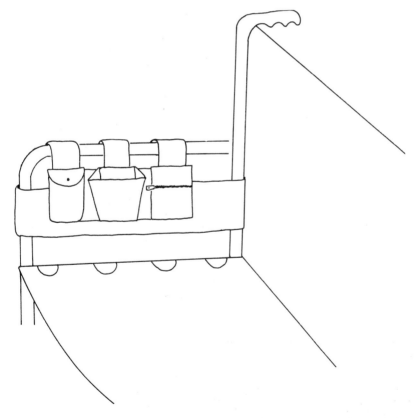

Figure 16. Pockets with various closures, attached to the inside of a wheelchair arm to keep things within easy reach.

reached, particularly for those with the use of only one hand. In addition to pockets on garments, or for use where there are no pockets on garments, pockets can be attached to waistline belts by providing one or two loops at the back of the pocket or just above the top of the pocket for the belts to pass through. Pockets, so attached, can be moved to the right or left for the convenience of the individual. For those who spend most of their time in wheelchairs, pockets can also be hung over the arms of wheelchairs with the pocket openings on the inside of the arms, so that things which may be needed can be within easy reach.

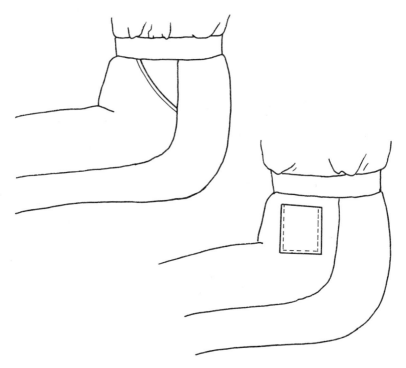

Figure 17. Front trouser pocket located parallel to the waistline or in a diagonal line from waistline to side seam for easier reach when seated in a wheelchair.

Trouser pockets in side seams are difficult to reach from a sitting position. Pockets placed parallel to the waistline or in a slanting position from the waistline to the side seams are easier to reach. For the sitting position, pockets cannot be as deep as for the standing position, and in custom-made trousers or those made at home, there should be no back pockets. In ready-made trousers, patch pockets in back may be removed. When trousers or slacks are worn which do not have pockets, the jacket, shirt, or other top garment should have usable pockets.

Clothing for the Sitting Position

Most clothing is proportioned for the standing position rather than the sitting position, and because wheelchair users are likely to spend much time in the sitting position, some adjustments can be made to increase comfort and improve appearance. Trousers and slacks need a high rise in the back and a lower rise in the front, to avoid the feeling of dropping down in back and bunching up in front. Patterns for making trousers can be altered to provide for this adjustment and custom-made trousers can be proportioned to accommodate to the sitting position. Ready-made trousers can be altered by inserting a piece of rib knit fabric in matching color in the back between the band and the top of the trousers, and lowering the front of the trousers below the band. The insert should be widest at the center back and tapered to the side seams. The lowering of the front of the trousers involves the removal of the zipper in the fly and inserting a shorter zipper or Velcro, but it does not

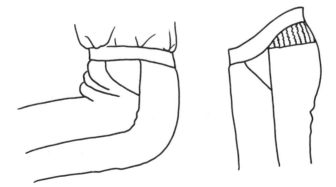

Figure 18. Trousers with a high rise in the back and a low rise in the front to accommodate the sitting position for those confined to wheelchairs.

involve any changes at the side seams. The lowering of the front rise will be deepest at the center front, tapering to the side seams.[2,3]

Trousers and slacks are cut in the right length for the standing position rather than the sitting position; thus, in the sitting position, there is a gap between the end of the trousers or slacks and the ankles. Those made for wheelchair users should be longer, and ready-mades can be lengthened by dropping the cuffs and making shallow hems. On those without cuffs, hems can be dropped and the ends faced with fabric of matching color.

Just as trousers and slacks are not cut for the sitting position, neither are suit jackets. Those to be worn in wheelchairs need

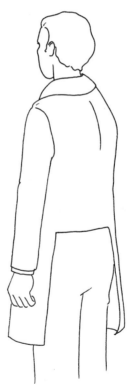

Figure 19. Coat with back, below the hips, cut away to provide for greater comfort in the sitting position for those confined to wheelchairs.

to be cut shorter in the front to avoid bunching up in front, and to avoid a roll developing just below the collar in the back, there needs to be less length in the back of the jacket from the neckline to the hipline. The end of the jacket back should reach only to the seat of the chair. Vents at the side seams from four to six inches long, improve the appearance of the front of the jacket. Jackets proportioned for the sitting position must either be custom-made or made at home by adjusting patterns accordingly.

For those who spend much time seated in wheelchairs outdoors full length coats can be burdensome and uncomfortabe. To make a coat less burdensome, more comfortable, and easier to arrange the front of the coat in a straight easy position, the back of the coat below the hips can be cut away and an appropriate finish applied to the cut edges. Custom-made coats may be ordered without backs below the hips. One other advantage of coats without backs below the hips is that they can be put on and taken off while the wearer is in a sitting position. Coats may be made with a zipper or Velcro up the back seam for ease in putting on and taking off the coat for those with a nonfunctional arm.[2, 4]

Dresses and skirts worn by women who use wheelchairs should be long enough to cover the knees and wide enough to be comfortable, but not so wide as to interfere in propelling the chair. Very full skirts, which may be in fashion at times, could get caught in the wheels. In the relaxed sitting position in wheelchairs, there must be some provision for waistline adjustment. Rather than fitted waistlines on dresses by means of darts, dresses may be made without waistline fitting, may be elasticized at the waistline, or simply fitted with tie belts. Provision for waistline adjustment in wrap-style dresses may be made by using Velcro as the fastening, in lengths long enough to make necessary adjustments for comfort.

Wrap-style skirts adapt easily to the needs of wheelchair users. Wrapped at the back, adjustable waistline ties can be used or Velcro can be used as the waistline fastening. To give the appearance of a button waistline closure, a button can be sewn over the Velcro at the end of a skirt band. Long wrap-style

Figure 20. Coat and jacket with zipper or Velcro closure in the center back seam for ease in putting on and taking off for those with a nonfunctional arm.

skirts provide complete coverage and are especially suitable for travel. To avoid bunching up below the waistline, skirts can be cut a little lower at the center front, tapering out to the side seams, and the back of the skirt can be shortened to reach only to the seat of the chair rather than full length. The best fastening at the ends of the skirt band would be ties or Velcro attached to the skirt band. A skirt of this kind could be put on and taken off in the sitting position.

Two-piece dresses have advantages for women who use wheelchairs. One-piece dresses tend to bunch up above and below the waistline because they are generally cut for the standing position. Blouses and other tops worn with skirts are better worn over skirts than tucked in to provide a neater appearance, since reaching changes the position of the tucked-in blouse or other top at some places. For those worn over skirts, a smoother appearance can sometimes be achieved by making four to six inch vents or plackets at the side seams, such as are seen on men's sport shirts and jackets which are worn with trousers and slacks. Jackets worn with dresses, skirts, and slacks should be only long enough to reach the seat of the chair in back rather than longer lengths which do not fit as smoothly in a sitting position.

THE MENTALLY RETARDED

Clothing problems of the mentally retarded may be broadly grouped as (1) the need for protection, (2) ease in dressing and undressing, and (3) control of deviant behavior in regard to clothing. One of the most important factors in protection concerns fire hazards. Mentally retarded individuals may be unaware of danger and slow in reaction time, and one form of protection is the use of flame-retardant fabrics for outer garments. For those who have problems of balance and fall easily or who are subject to convulsive disorders, head injuries can be avoided by the use of protective headgear designed to fit the head. Further detail on protective headgear appears in Chapter 8.

Some mentally retarded individuals, with other physical problems, have no feeling in certain parts of their bodies, and for them, smooth surfaces on their clothing are important in order to avoid skin irritations; there should be no excessive tightness of clothing or of elastic which is used in clothing.

Some, who have normal feeling and high pain tolerance, may suffer pain and not know what to do about it. For this reason, safety pins, which may open, should not be used in the clothing of mentally retarded children.

Among the profoundly and severely retarded, the problems of constant drooling requires protection for clothing. The best protection is absorbent bibs with separate plastic linings so that bibs can be laundered. For some children, bibs may need frequent changing. The easiest way to put bibs on is with ties at the back of the neck. If garments are made at home, bibs can be made to go with the garments, using absorbent fabric such as terry cloth in the same color as the garment fabric. Two small loops of the garment fabric can be attached to the garment

Figure 21. Bibs attached with Velcro or ties at the shoulders to protect clothing from constant drooling.

where the shoulder seam meets the neckline and midway between the neckline and the end of the shoulder seam. Ties can then be attached to the bibs at the same places so that the bibs can be tied to the loops. When the drooling problem is not very severe, bibs made of the garment fabric may be attached to the garment with Velcro. Such bibs are the least conspicuous. Disposable bibs are available and are especially convenient to use when children who drool are traveling or are otherwise away from home.

Another problem, common to the profoundly and severely retarded, is incontinence, which may continue throughout the whole lifetime. This condition requires the use of protective moisture-proof garments with inner absorbent padding of the diaper type, which may be either launderable or disposable. Those who are cared for by others are taken to the bathroom at intervals but must always wear protective garments. Beside protective garments of the diaper type, those subject to incontinence should have outer wear which is easily laundered and is stain resistant to cope with the frequent soiling of outer garments with urine and feces.[5] In areas where the profoundly and severely handicapped spend much time, the floors should be covered with linoleum rather than carpeting and the furniture should be covered with plastic materials rather than upholstery fabrics in order to avoid stains and odors which are difficult or impossible to completely remove. Problems of incontinence are further discussed in Chapter 8.

Dressing and Undressing

Independence in the activities of daily living, such as dressing and undressing, is very important for the mentally retarded. This not only provides an opportunity to exercise the initiative of which they may be capable and to take some responsibility for themselves, but it also eliminates the need for having someone else to do the dressing and undressing. In institutions, this procedure can be costly, and at home, it becomes time-consuming and burdensome for the person who must take the responsibility. Thus, all design features that can make dressing and undressing easier should be incorporated in garments for the mentally retarded.

One characteristic of the mentally retarded is slowness in learning, which may be apparent in learning to dress and undress. To simplify the process, closures on garments should be as easy as possible to manage and should be within easy reach. One-piece garments with front openings are generally easier to manage than two-piece garments which may have two kinds of closures. Those that need to be tied in a bow or knot or buckles that need to be fastened require learning and manipulation that may be beyond the abilities of some retarded individuals. The same is true of shoe closures, so shoes with no closures at all, with elastic sections in the sides which slip on and off with little effort, are the easiest to handle.

Garments that need to be put on over the head create problems for retarded individuals because of the reaching which is necessary and also the inability to distinguish the front from the back of the garment. A spot of color or mark of some kind can be used to distinguish the front from the back, which must be learned. Even this might be difficult for those with a very short memory span. In garments with sleeves, deeply cut armholes make it easier to dress and undress, and sleeves can be made wide enough to get the hands through without cuffs or wrist bands which must fasten.

Clothing Related to Deviant Behavior

For the mentally retarded individual who engages in deviant behavior, one of the most important considerations in clothing is the durability of the fabrics used for outer garments. The best choices are strong fabrics such as denim and corduroy. In addition to choice of fabric, construction processes used can add to the durability of garments. Seams should be double-stitched, and the best seam to use is the flat fell seam. All seam ends should be reinforced so that seams cannot be pulled apart at any places on garments, and there should be nothing on garments that can be torn off and cause damage to the garment such as buttons or loops for belts. Beside the reinforcements

generally needed at points of greatest wear, additional reinforcements are needed for mentally retarded children who crawl
or move about in a sitting position on concrete floors. No
fabric is completely abrasion resistant, so reinforcements must
be constantly renewed, especially at the seat area, knees, and
elbows.[5]

One form of deviant behavior is that of chewing and disinte-
grating garments. This may be controlled through choice of
garment design so that no part of the garment can be reached
for chewing. Disrobing is another form of deviant behavior,
and the best way to prevent it is to provide jump suits with
back zippers that lock at the top of the zipper and cannot be
opened by the wearer. Among the forms of deviant behavior
frequently found in profoundly and severely retarded children
is that of coprophilia, which is abnormal attraction to feces. In
this form of behavior, the child works his hands into the diapered area and spreads the fecal material on himself and on the
surfaces in his surroundings such as the floor, tables, and
chairs. To prevent coprophilia, the best type of garment is a
jump suit with one long zipper either in the front or back
which cannot be opened by the wearer, with pant legs too
narrow to push up and permit passage of the hand into the
diapered area in an effort to remove the diaper and reach the
feces. Since this behavior can also occur at night, the same type
of garment must be used for night wear, made of lighter weight
fabric. The problems of coprophilia requires the use of
moisture-proof diaper-type garments at all times.[5]

CHRONICALLY ILL

The chronically ill, especially among the aged, may have
some of the same needs as those with physical handicaps and
may also have some needs in relation to circulatory conditions.
Where there are circulatory problems, attention should be given
to elastic used in girdles and garters and in garments with
elasticized waistlines. No elastic should be constricting or cause
any discomfort.

Many of the chronically ill do not move about very frequently during the day and remain in a sitting position much of the time, so clothing should be comfortable and adapted to the sitting position. Clothing, in general, should be made of lightweight fabrics and soft textures to avoid irritation to the skin. For persons with little physical energy, the process of dressing and undressing should be accomplished with as much ease as possible. This calls for front openings that are easy to see and to reach, fastenings that are easy to manipulate, deep cut armholes, and extended or enlarged openings, especially for those with limited range of motion.

Garments for daytime wear for persons living in their own homes or in nursing homes should have pockets to keep needed things within easy reach and to avoid having to make many trips back to other rooms for things they need. Clothing, in general, should be easy to take care of, and for those residing in nursing homes, clothing should be identified with the name of the owner and should withstand institutional laundering. Those who are bedridden either at home or in nursing homes have little need for daytime wear, but those who are ambulatory should have daytime clothing in order to avoid the temptation of not getting up in the morning and staying in bed very much of the time during the day.[6]

EFFECTS OF PHYSICAL CHANGES ON CLOTHING NEEDS OF THE ELDERLY

Physical changes that occur in the process of aging are gradual, and though all people are affected in time, the rate and the onset of physical changes are different for all people. In our age-conscious society, however, the physical indications of increasing age are readily recognized.

Changes in Stature and Body Contour

For many people, there is a loss in height caused by a progressive shortening of the spinal column, and for some, there is a bending of the spinal column that appears as a curve on the upper back. This back contour has a tendency to pull up the back of garments and distort the appearance of the waistline and the hemline of garments. The use of half-size dresses is one way to accommodate to the loss of height. Half-sizes are usually one inch shorter in the bodice and one inch shorter in the skirt. Ready-made garments do not fit the figure with a back curve, but garments can be made to fit the figure. Pattern alteration for this condition appears in Chapter 6.

One of the physical changes that occurs in older people is the shifting of body fat, which changes the contour of the body and of the face. One of the most noticeable changes in body contour is the expansion of the abdomen and the hips. When this occurs, often the legs get thinner which makes it difficult to keep hosiery fitted to the legs without wrinkles. Though some people lose weight and become very thin in their late years, those who gain weight are more numerous. Those who gain weight find that dresses without fitted waistlines accommodate to the larger figure better than those with fitted waistlines. With much added weight, the waistline almost disappears. When older men gain weight, their trousers need to be larger in the waistline to fit the enlarged abdomen and also, their coats need more room in the waistline area.[7]

As changes in the facial contour occur, the cheekbones, nose, ears, and lips become more prominent as the face thins out. Facial wrinkles appear: vertical folds from the ends of the mouth to the nose, sometimes called *parentheses,* horizontal wrinkles on the forehead, and vertical wrinkles between the eyebrows. When such changes occur, the softening effect of clothing, especially in the neckline area, detracts from the facial contours and makes the person appear more attractive. When these physical changes take place, which may be as early as the fifties, the skin becomes dry, thin, and inelastic and subject to irritation by coarse textures and rough places on garments. Thus, fabric becomes important in the choice of clothing, and soft textured, lightweight fabrics provide the greatest comfort.[7]

Changes in Physical Strength and Muscle Tone

Other physical conditions that accompany aging and affect

clothing needs are reduced physical strength and limited reach and range of motion. These conditions bring about the need for front openings on garments so that garments do not have to be put on over the head, nor does the wearer have to reach to the back of the garment, which is difficult for people of all ages. Also, fastenings on garments should be easy to manipulate, such as Velcro, zippers equipped with rings for easy grasp, and large buttons. Very small buttons and hooks and eyes that require greater finger dexterity should be avoided.

Shifting of body fat and loss of muscle tone often brings about the sagging of arm muscles which makes the arms less attractive. Thus, many older women dislike sleeveless or very short-sleeved fashions in dresses, blouses, and sweaters. For informal wear or sportswear, they find slacks preferable to shorts which would reveal loss of muscle tone in sagging leg muscles. As the body loses muscle tone, the bustline becomes less accentuated. The breasts become elongated and flattened and the figure no longer fits into garments with a high well-defined bustline. When these figure changes take place, the darts that shape the bodice should be of the right size and in the right location on the garment to accommodate the figure.

SAFETY FACTORS IN THE SELECTION AND USE OF CLOTHING AND FOOTWEAR BY THE ELDERLY

Injuries to older people that involve clothing and footwear are often those which result from falls and burns. The National Safety Council reports that falls are the number one killer in the home today and, next to traffic accidents, are the largest single cause of accidental injury and death each year in the United States. Falls are especially frequent among people age sixty-five and over, and although people in this age group comprise only 9 or 10 percent of the population, they account for 80 percent of the fatal falls at home. The incidence of injury and death from falls is even higher among those age seventy-five and over. When hospitalized for fall injuries, they require about twice the length of time for treatment and recovery as do people in other age groups, particularly when severe head injuries and broken bones are involved. The incidence of injury and death from fire and burns among the elderly is also very high for those age sixty-five to seventy-four and higher than those in any younger age group. For those seventy-five and older, it is the highest. Recovery from severe burns is a very long process and many of the elderly do not survive.[8,9]

Falls Caused by Clothing

In selecting clothing and footwear, the factors most people consider to be of greatest importance are fashion, newness, aesthetic values, and price because of the social connotations of these factors. However, safety factors are of utmost importance in the clothing and footwear of older people and should be given highest priority. In order to lessen the possibility of falls caused by clothing, certain design features should be avoided. Belts, ties, and sashes on dresses, robes, and other garments worn at home should not be so long that the ends could easily be stepped on and cause the wearer to fall. They should be secured at some place on the waistline so that one end cannot hang down to the floor. When younger people suddenly feel themselves slipping, they have a greater chance of regaining their balance instead of falling, but many older people lack muscular control and the slightest little slip results in a fall.

Full length robes, negligees, and housecoats that reach almost to the floor are in fashion at times, but they are hazardous for older people. Those who walk with a shuffling gait instead of lifting their feet are in danger of stepping on the lower edge of such garments and falling. Also, when the wearer fails to fasten the garment in front and bends forward to stand from a sitting position, it is very easy to step on the end of the garment and fall. Garments with flowing panels and deep kimono sleeves can also be hazardous as they get caught and throw the wearer. Such garments can get caught in room doors as they are being closed, in elevator doors and car doors, and even in refrigerator doors, bureau drawers, and suitcases. Full-length sleeves that are fitted or otherwise narrow in design are safer. Three-quarter sleeves that come to within a few inches of the wrist may be fuller without the risk of getting caught or the risk of falling.

Another design feature that can cause falls is pockets positioned low at the sides of garments, including skirts, dresses, and coats. Such pockets that are open at the outside edge can catch on door knobs, especially bar-shaped door knobs often found on screen doors and some car doors. Pockets should be so located on dresses and coats that they will not come in contact with door knobs or other projections. Pockets that open at the top instead of the side present no problem.

Older women often wear sweaters indoors for extra warmth, and the manner of wearing their sweaters can be hazardous rather than the sweaters themselves. If the sweaters are difficult to put on over the sleeves of dresses or blouses, they are sometimes worn draped over the shoulders in stole or shawl fashion and possibly fastened at the neck. With the sleeves dangling, they could get caught somewhere and cause a fall. Sweaters to be worn indoors over dresses or blouses should have deep-cut armholes and full-cut sleeves to avoid the temptation of wearing them draped over the shoulders.

Current fashions for women are not completely ignored by older women and many older women wear slacks and pantsuits. When these garments first became fashionable for women, they were styled like men's trousers, and later, variations appeared in the width of legs and depth of cuffs. When wide legs and deep cuffs are in fashion, they should not be selected by older women because a foot can easily get caught in the opposite cuff or in the fullness of the leg, as with very long full skirts, and cause a fall. Even younger people experience these difficulties.

Falls Caused by Footwear

Foot problems are common to many older people, which in turn, create problems in the selection and use of footwear. Shoes should fit properly and be comfortable. Those whose feet hurt from pressure in some places are often tempted to buy shoes that are too large, which may result in a shuffling motion in walking that can cause falls. Those who have special needs should not prescribe for themselves, but should have the advice of a qualified podiatrist. When the pressure of shoes at some one place on the foot becomes very severe, the pain of just walking can cause falls. For greatest general comfort, shoes should be made of soft leather or other soft material to accommodate the shape of the foot rather than more rigid material in a larger size.

For those who have to walk on hard finish floors such as tile, linoleum, or polished wood, slick soles on shoes or slippers can cause sudden slipping and falls. Under these conditions, slick soles should be avoided. Adequate footwear to accommodate these conditions is very important, not only to avoid falls while wearing shoes or slippers, but to avoid the temptation of walking in stocking feet which is much the same as walking in slick soled footwear. Walking up and down wooden stairs in stocking feet is especially hazardous.

Many older women wear oxford type shoes that require shoe laces. Shoes that lace are not hazardous in themselves, but often the shoes are worn unlaced or untied with the laces dangling because the wearer either forgets to tie them or cannot bend down to reach the laces: Stepping on dangling laces can cause falls; also, the unlaced shoes can be so loose that they come off in walking and cause the wearer to lose balance and fall. Those who want to wear lace shoes and have difficulty in tying them might find it advantageous to use elastic laces which stay laced and tied and have enough stretch so the shoes can be put on and taken off while the shoes remain laced and tied.

Slippers worn indoors provide comfort but may cause the wearer to fall if, in seeking comfort, the slippers worn are a bit too large and loose and could come off in walking. Also, slippers without backs, called mules, create the same falling hazard. If they do not fit snugly, they may fall off and cause the wearer to stumble and fall. In going up and down steps, slippers without backs are especially hazardous. In an effort to keep the slippers on, the toes flex and as the foot goes down, the toe grasp is lessened and the wearer is likely to fall.[10]

Some older women are inclined to be conservative in relation to new fashions and others are eager to try what is new. Among the footwear fashions that are especially hazardous are the high platform shoes that also have high heels, the clogs without backs, wedge style shoes, and very loosely fitted sandals. In wearing platform shoes, the normal reflex pattern of walking is affected by the rigidity of the thick soles and the stiltlike walk. People of all ages who wear platform shoes experience severe falls. Wedges and clogs lack flexibility and must fit very snugly to stay on. Sandals that fit loosely provide no support or stability, can change positions on the feet while walking, and can cause falls.

Burns that Involve Clothing

Next to falls, burns account for the largest number of accidental deaths, and almost half of them involve clothing. Older people are slower in reaction time than younger people, often resulting in greater severity of burns and longer periods of hospitalization. Design of clothing is a major consideration in lessening the possibility of injuries and death from burn accidents. When a garment is ignited, the immediate impulse is to get the garment off as quickly as possible, and those that are easy to get off may lessen the degree of injury from burns. Garments with flowing panels and long sleeves that are very full at the ends or that have oversize decoration cuffs are hazardous near open flames such as gas ranges and candles and cause frequent burn injuries. Also, dangling sleeves on sweaters or robes worn in cape style are equally hazardous around open flames. Garments worn in the kitchen while preparing food should have no excess fullness or dangling parts that could easily come in contact with flames or hot surfaces on a gas or electric range. Many accidents occur in reaching over the top of the range to a back burner and also in leaning against the range for warmth.[11]

Another very important factor, in addition to design of clothing, is the use of nonflammable fabrics for some garments under certain conditions. Those older people who retain the habit of smoking should wear clothing made of nonflammable fabric for their own protection insofar as it is possible to purchase such clothing or have it made. In striking a match, the smoker may lose his grip on the match and it may fall on clothing, or in disposing of the lighted match, the smoker may miss the ash tray and the lighted match may fall on clothing. Sometimes, in striking a match, a small part of the match tip may separate from the match and land on clothing and ignite.

Beside the burns that can result from dropped matches when the smoker is awake, very serious burn injuries can result from the smoker falling asleep holding a lighted cigarette that finally falls on clothing, upholstery, carpeting or, bedding. Older people who smoke in bed run a great risk of falling asleep with lighted cigarettes in their hands which could fall on their night clothes or the bedding. Those who smoke in bed should take the precaution of wearing only nonflammable night clothes and should use only nonflammable bedding insofar as it is possible to obtain it.

Many burn accidents occur among older rural people in the process of burning trash, leaves, and brush. In their efforts to control the fires, they get too close and the flames ignite their clothing, or flying sparks light on their clothing and ignite. In windy weather, outdoor fires can be especially hazardous. With flames shooting high in the air, the fire builders may watch the top of the flames without being aware of what is happening on the ground and how fast the fire is spreading. Standing near a fire one expects to feel some warmth, and when the ignited clothing is discovered, the fire may be well under way, causing a severe injury. Some older people may seek to hasten the process of fire building by using gasoline or other flammable liquids, and in pouring it on the fire, they may get some of it on themselves, particularly on trouser legs. When they succeed in getting the fire started, they may stand so close that the gasoline on their clothing ignites in a flash. The use of nonflammable clothing would remove at least one of the hazards of fire building, even with the use of flammable fire starters.[12]

REFERENCES

1. *The Fascinating Story of Fasteners.* New York, Velcro Educational Services, Velcro Corporation.

2. Cookman, Helen and Zimmerman, Muriel: *Functional Fashions for the Physically Handicapped.* New York Institute of Physical Medicine and Rehabilitation, New York University Medical Center, 1961.

3. Bowar, Mariam T.: *Clothing for the Handicapped — Fashion Adaptations for Adults and Children.* Minneapolis, Sister Kenny Institute, 1977.

4. *Men's Fashions for the Wheelchair Set.* Chicago, Leinenweber, Inc.

5. Hallenbeck, Phyllis N. and Behrens, Dorothy A.: Clothing problems of the retarded. *Mental Retardation,* 5(1):21-24, February, 1967.

6. Hoffman, Adeline M.: Clothing: social and therapeutic values. In Jacobs, H. Lee, and Morris, W. W. (Eds.): *Nursing and Retirement Home Administration.* Ames, Iowa State U, 1966.

7. Tate, Mildred Thurow and Glisson, Oris: *Family Clothing.* New York, Wiley, 1961.

8. *Accidents to the Elderly — Age 65 and Over.* National Safety Council, 1973.

9. *Accident Facts — 1977 Final condensed Edition.* National Safety Council, August, 1977.

10. Agate, John: Accidents to old people. *Community Health,* 2(1):27-35, July-August, 1970.

11. Mersdorf, Doris: How to protect the elderly. *Home Safety Review,* 20-24, Winter, 1959.

12. Piercy, Larry R.: *Clothing Burn Injuries of Rural Residents.* Paper presented at 1971 Winter meeting of American Society of Agricultural Engineers, Chicago.

Chapter 6

SOURCES OF CLOTHING TO
MEET SPECIAL NEEDS

THE three major sources of clothing to meet
special needs are (1) clothing specially designed for the physically handicapped, (2) ready-made clothing adapted to meet the
needs of the individual, and (3) clothing made at home by a
family member or by a local dressmaker or tailor to meet the
needs of the individual.

SPECIALLY DESIGNED CLOTHING

Specially designed clothing for the physically handicapped is
available by mail order from a number of sources, some of
which appear in the Appendix. Garments are described and
illustrated in mail order catalogs and instructions are given, in
most catalogs, for taking measurements of the person for whom
the garments are ordered, to insure correct fit. A few catalogs
include samples of fabrics. Some people engaged in the specially designed garment business make garments for stock in
regular sizes and others only make garments to measure for
their individual customers. Those in this business serve a very
important need and must cope with the problem of catering to
an uncertain market. This market is difficult to identify and
equally difficult to reach, and the same variables exist in this
market as in the general clothing market. However, production
for those with special needs is further complicated by the various kinds, degrees, and combinations of disabilities for which
clothing must be adapted.

SELECTION OF READY-MADE CLOTHING

In selecting ready-made clothing for persons with special
needs, consideration must be given to the individual's physical

limitations including muscle strength, reach and range of motion, eye-hand coordination, grasp, and finger dexterity. Garments selected should provide for ease in dressing and undressing, should be adaptable to the use of braces, crutches, and wheelchairs, should fit well and be comfortable, and should also be attractive. It is highly desirable to take to the store those persons for whom garments are to be purchased in order to given them the opportunity to make selections. In special cases, appointments may be made with store managers, in some communities, for handicapped persons who might require much time of sales people to come either before or after hours. Garments considered for purchase should always be tried on for fit, comfort, and general appearance and should be checked in both sitting and standing positions, in motion, and in reaching and raising arms. This is especially important for those who may spend much of their time sitting and may need greater length in skirts and slacks. In the process of trying on, determination should be made of the possibility for putting on and taking off without help.

When the person for whom a garment is being purchased cannot be present to try on the garment, it is important for the purchaser to have a list of body measurements and ease allowances or the dimensions of a garment that fits the person, in order to select a garment which will fit and to avoid the need to return the garment for a different size or a refund. Some things to look for in garments generally are (1) enough room for ease of motion, (2) nonrestricting sleeves such as raglan and kimono styles, (3) garment openings to facilitate ease in dressing and undressing, (4) buttons and other fasteners of size and kind appropriate to the finger dexterity and grasp of the individual, and (5) other features according to the specific needs of the individual.

Ready-made garments frequently require adaptations, so garments should be checked to determine the possibility of making needed adaptations. Among the things which should be checked are seam width, hem depth, placement of darts, and whether or not darts have been trimmed to seam width, making it impossible to relocate them. For adaptations that involve the need for more fabric, such as adding action pleats or widening sleeves, it would be helpful, before purchasing the garment, to determine whether or not fabric would be available that would combine well with the garment fabric in making changes to adapt to needs. Those with body contours and proportions which deviate very much from standard cut and sizes may require much adapting and the need for additional fabric.

Garments of classic design, which are not dated, are a much better choice for most people than current fashion which soon may become obviously old. However, among those physically handicapped individuals who must be in daily contact with the public, there is a need to look like other people, and for them, fashion-rightness becomes another essential factor in the selection of clothing.

In the purchasing of ready-made garments for aged persons and those residing in nursing homes, they should also be taken to stores to select garments and to try them on, if it is possible. If they are unable to go to the stores, those assisting them in their purchases should bring a number of garments from the stores from which they could make choices. This would give them an opportunity to make final selection and exercise more control over their lives than being totally dependent on the ideas, opinions, and prerogatives of other persons. Local stores generally allow customers to take out garments on approval in making purchases for those who cannot come to the stores. Relatives and friends, who send or bring clothing items as gifts, should be sure they will be useful and appropriate in terms of size, fit, comfort, ease of care, and that they will be within the interests, tastes, and needs of the recipients. Also, they should know the physical limitations of those for whom they purchase clothing items.

One of the reasons children give for their preference of ready-made garments, which might have to be altered, rather than those made at home is their strong desire to have clothes like those worn by other children. Clothes that children like make them happy and self-confident. In the selection, children should be given some opportunity for choice in order to give them a sense of responsibility for themselves. In providing ready-made clothing, parents sometimes buy a larger size in some garments to fit over braces, which might make other parts of such garments too large and create discomfort. Good fit is important to insure comfort, facilitate mobility, and provide a feeling of being well-dressed. Garments that do not fit well may get caught somewhere and cause a child to fall.

Young children grow at a rapid rate and soon outgrow their clothes. Design features to look for in purchasing clothing for young children are those that counteract this problem, such as raglan sleeves. Raglan sleeves provide ease and allowance for growth, while garments with set-in sleeves are more quickly outgrown. In dresses for girls, designs without waistlines and with deep hems adapt to growth. Other features to look for in children's garments are long front openings or large overhead openings, expandable necklines, and easy-to-manage fastenings in order to simplify the process of dressing and undressing. Consideration must also be given to the specific physical limitations, as in the selection of garments for adults. In selecting slacks or jeans in which an opening must be made in leg seams to accommodate braces, it is best to select those with plain seams instead of fell seams for greater ease in inserting zippers or Velcro.

ADAPTATION OF READY-MADE CLOTHING

Physically handicapped and elderly people have some clothing needs that can be met by simple adaptations of ready-made clothing. Many may require more than one kind of adaptation, some of which may be more complicated and time-consuming than others. While many of the adaptations suggested are for the purpose of convenience and wear-resistance, others are directly related to physical limitations concerned mainly with range of motion, paralysis, grasp, finger dexterity, general muscular weakness, and the use of braces, crutches, prostheses, and wheelchairs.

Adaptations for the Physically Handicapped

Some adaptations suggested for the physically handicapped

are also applicable to elderly people who may have some age-related disabilities, chronic illnesses, or physical conditions which create limitations in the use of clothing.

Fastenings and Location of Openings

Garments that open in the back, with zippers from the neckline to below the waistline, are often difficult to manipulate for people who lack strength in their hands or whose range of motion is so limited that they are unable to reach the zippers. According to the design of the dress, it is sometimes possible to remove the back zipper, make an opening in the front of the dress, and insert with the zipper mechanism exposed. This type of adaptation would be somewhat limited by the total design of the garment, especially the neckline. Such a change could not be made very easily on a garment with a collar that opened in the back, unless the collar was removed and turned to open in the front or was replaced with a facing or other appropriate neckline finish. When the problem of manipulating a zipper in the back of a garment is only a matter of gripping the zipper pull, a large ring, about an inch in diameter, can be inserted in the zipper pull which would make it much easier to grasp in opening and closing the zipper. In this case, it would not be necessary to change the location of the zipper from the back to the front of the garment.

For women who have difficulty in reaching the back fastening of bras, the adaptation from back to front opening is fairly simple, especially if the bra is constructed with a center front seam. Bra "repair packages" are available in stores where sewing supplies are sold and include directions and materials for making front openings. The back opening must be permanently closed as an opening is made at the center front, adding an extension on the left edge of the opening and a facing on the right edge. Either hooks and eyes or Velcro may be used as the fastening. Bras made with center front openings are available at many stores and from a number of mail order catalogs.

The adaptation for those who lack the ability to handle small button closures is to remove the small buttons and sew them on over the buttonholes as they would appear when the garment was buttoned. Then small blocks of Velcro should be sewn on where the buttons were and blocks of the other side of the Velcro tape should be sewn under the buttonholes. The method of fastening the garment would then be merely getting the Velcro patches lined up and pressed together. Velcro is called "pressure tape" because of the action that is needed to bring the two sides of the Velcro together when used in closures. With limited flexion of the fingers and the wrist, Velcro is easier to use than most other fasteners. Another adaptation to make some small buttons easier to handle is the use of longer thread shanks or elastic thread for sewing on buttons.

The most frequent adaptations on trousers and slacks are the replacement of buttons at the waistbands with large trouser hooks or Velcro, and the insertion of zippers in the side seams to adapt to the use of braces and the use of urinal bags, to provide ease in dressing, and to permit the seat section or the top front section to drop for ease in toileting. This adaptation requires the addition of an inner belt attached to the waistband to hold the garment in place while one section is dropped.

Pockets

Pockets on garments are especially needed by those among the physically handicapped and also the elderly who must always have keys and other things at hand and who have problems of mobility. The easiest type of pocket to add to ready-made garments is the patch pocket. On women's dresses and skirts, pockets may also be made in the side seams. Fabric used for patch pockets may be used for additional trim within the possibilities of the garment design. Pockets in side seams show very little, so fabric used is of lesser importance but should be compatible with the color and weight of the garment fabric. On men's garments, some pockets may need to be relocated for easier use though there are usually enough pockets, but pockets may need to be added on children's and women's garments. Patch pockets on the backs of trousers and slacks which are uncomfortable for men confined to wheelchairs should be removed, and pockets in a position easier to reach and, therefore, more useful should be added. For those who use crutches, inside pockets may be added to coats to guard against losses from open shallow pockets on the outside of coats, which also may be awkward to reach.

Sleeves

The sleeve adaptation for those who use crutches is to relieve the strain on long sleeves that are narrow at the wrist or finished with fitted bands. Such sleeves need to be shortened to about midway between the wrist and the elbow. Sleeves on outer garments such as jackets and coats are usually wide

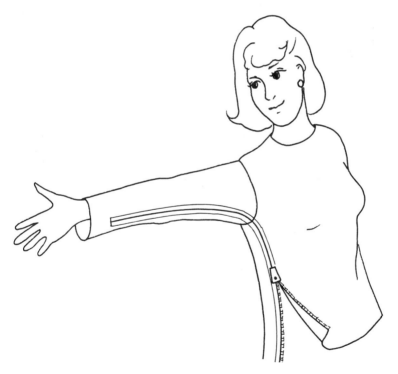

Figure 22. Zipper inserted in sleeve and side seam of a garment for greater ease in dressing for those with a paralyzed arm.

enough to withstand the pull of the crutches.

For those with a paralyzed arm which is difficult to insert in a sleeve, the sleeve seam and underarm seam of the garment can be opened and a zipper inserted. The open sleeve area would make it easier to put the garment on and the zipper closures would not be difficult to manipulate. Another adaptation for greater ease in inserting a paralyzed arm in a sleeve of a jacket or coat is to open the center back seam and insert Velcro or a zipper so that the jacket or coat can be put on more easily. This adaptation also serves the needs of those with both arms paralyzed who require assistance in dressing.

Neckties

Men who have limited range of motion or the use of just one hand are usually unable to put on neckties that need to be tied in knots or bows. For those with this limitation, an adaptation is to tie the knots or bows permanently, and then most of the part of the tie that goes around the neck can be eliminated, leaving only about three inches on each side of the bow or knot. The raw edges can be finished to prevent fraying and Velcro can then be sewn to the inside edges of the neckline ends to fasten to Velcro pieces sewn to the neckline of the shirt so that the tie can be put in place easily, even with one hand. This adaptation can be made on purchased ties and those already in the wardrobe of the person with this need. Another adaptation for putting on ties with one hand is to tie or knot the tie permanently, eliminate most of the part that goes around the neck and substitute elastic so that the tie will stay in place and be comfortable.

Limited Reach

Many of the clothing adaptations suggested are concerned with greater ease in dressing. Some physically handicapped persons with lower extremity paralysis and limited reach have difficulty in putting on trousers, slacks, socks, and stockings. For those who dress in bed, loops of tape or fabric can be attached to the tops of trousers and slacks, which can be reached with hooks at the ends of long dowel sticks. The trousers or slacks can be pulled on over the knees, and then with the raising of the buttocks, they can be pulled on the rest of the way. Loops attached to the tops of socks or stockings can be used in the same way in pulling them on when the tops of socks or stockings cannot be reached with the hands.

Sitting Position

For those who spend much time outdoors in wheelchairs, there is an adaptation that can make coats more comfortable and improve their appearance. The back section, from the seat of the wheelchair to the end of the coat, can be eliminated to avoid the discomfort of sitting on folds of heavy coat fabric. This makes the buttoned coat appear to fit better instead of bunching up in the front. Also, a coat, so adapted, can be put on and taken off in the sitting position. Trousers, slacks, and skirts have a tendency to ride up in the sitting position, so they need to be longer. Slacks and trousers may be lengthened by dropping the cuffs or the hems and finishing the ends with facings. In skirts, hems can also be dropped and skirts can be finished with facings. One other adaptation to provide for better fitting of trousers or slacks in the sitting position is to raise the back and lower the front. This adaptation is described in the preceding chapter.

Reinforcement at Points of Wear

Before ready-made garments are worn, reinforcements should be added where they are needed. The fabric used should be stronger than the garment fabric and may be attached either by machine or by hand according to access to various places on garments. Elbows and knees are the usual places where reinforcements are needed, but there may be additional places according to the needs of the individual. To avoid abrasion at the knees of slacks or trousers for those who wear long leg braces, inverted pleats can be added at the knee area, and also lining can be added to avoid abrasion on the garment fabric.

In addition to adaptations concerned with abrasion, some seams should be reinforced. The curved section of underarm seams in kimono and raglan sleeves can be reinforced by clipping and pressing the seams open, covering with a single thickness of bias binding, pinning in place, and then stitching from the right side of the garment about one-eighth inch from each side of the sleeve seams.

Gussets

Sometimes more ease is needed in getting into sleeves in the process of dressing and in reaching when the garment is worn. To provide the additional ease, diamond-shaped gussets may be added under the arms. Those who use crutches may need gussets for comfort and to minimize wear on the garment itself. Such gussets should be made of fabric that matches the garment fabric as closely as possible in order to be inconspicuous. Gussets are functional additions to garments and are not meant to be decorative though they are sometimes in fashion because of the design of garments.

Other Adaptations

In some garments, other adaptations may be needed in accordance with the garment design and physical disabilities of various kinds, degrees, and combinations. Some needed adaptations can be determined by the physically handicapped person and the family member or other person who takes responsibility for the handicapped person's clothing. The understanding and ingenuity of such persons may supersede the knowledge of those who have analyzed clothing problems in the abstract but who lack the experience of those who have dealt with clothing problems over a long period of time.

Adaptations for the Elderly

Changes that occur in the physical body as a result of the

normal process of aging are described in the preceding chapter, and suggestions are given in regard to design and proportions to meet the needs of older people. While it is true that many individuals experience little change in body proportions from early adulthood to old age and, therefore, have few if any problems in finding suitable and well-fitting ready-made clothing, this is not true of the majority of older people. Among older people, some changes in body proportions do occur which make it difficult to find ready-made clothing that is appropriate in design and acceptable in fit.

Changes in Front Bodice Darts

Simple alterations can be made on some garments to improve the design and make the garments fit the figure. On the front bodice of dresses, the bustline darts may be too high and they may easily be lowered to fit the wearer if the dart fold lines have not been trimmed and if holes do not appear at the ends of the darts. In the cutting and marking process in ready-made garments, many manufacturers mark the end of the dart with an instrument that makes a small hole that would show if the dart was relocated. In darts that are wider than seam allowances, the dart folds are usually trimmed so they will be the same width as seam allowances in the garment. Darts which are not trimmed and marked with a hole at the end may be easily relocated to improve the fit of the garment. A dart that originates at the waistline and goes toward the bustline may be taken out and the fullness at the waistline replaced by gathers to better fit the figure with a low bustline.

Changes in Shoulder Length

Older people often find that shoulder lines are too long for them and the tops of set-in sleeves appear to drop over the end of their shoulders, making the garments look too large. To correct this condition, a very simple alteration may be made. A tuck may be made across the shoulder seam, three or four inches down the front and the back of the garment. The depth of such a tuck should be determined by how much extra length on the shoulder line needs to be taken up to bring the armseye line up to the tip of the shoulder. The fold of the tuck should reach the armseye line. This kind of tuck could also be made on the inside of the garment with the stitching line close to the armseye line with the tuck turned toward the neckline to form an inverted pleat next to the armseye line.

A method of correcting shoulder length without adding any fullness to the back of the garment would be to remove the sleeve cap, open a few inches of the shoulder seam, reduce the length of the back shoulder seam by recutting the back of the armseye and laying or stitching in the extra front shoulder length in a pleat. When the shoulder seam is sewn and the sleeve cap is sewn back in place, the edge of the pleat should reach to the armseye line. Another method for reducing the length of shoulder lines is to remove the sleeves, recut the armhole of the bodice both back and front, and sew the sleeves back in place. When a large change of this kind is made, it may be necessary to deepen the underarm seams slightly to make the sleeves fit the new armseye lines.

Waistline Changes

To increase the waistline of a dress with a fitted waistline, the simplest method is to release darts on both bodice and skirt if they are not trimmed and ends marked with holes. Gathers in the bodice waistline can be released; tucks or pleats in the skirt could be released, and the side seams could be reduced in width to provide more room in the waistline. These alterations might call for a longer belt or tie which could be made in a fabric of contrasting color or other fabric to coordinate with the color and design of the garment fabric. For the very slim figure with a small waistline, the garment waistline may have to be reduced. This may be achieved through the use of darts, tucks, gathers, pleats, or deepened side seams, according to the amount of reduction needed for the desired fit. If a reduction of four inches or more is needed, it may be more advisable to take the garment apart at the waistline and do the necessary refitting and recutting to accommodate the smaller size in order for the garment to not appear too large in other dimensions even though the waistline had been scaled down.

When wide stiff belts are in fashion, which may not be appropriate for the person with a large waistline, a soft tie belt may be made of a fabric that would be appropriate in color and texture with the garment fabric. Not only does a wide stiff belt call attention to the waistline, but it may be difficult to fasten and adjust to changes in the waistline girth. A soft tie belt would be more easily adjustable, less conspicuous, and might be easier to handle for those with problems of grasp and finger dexterity.

Neckline Changes

Some women who are stout and have very short necks prefer dresses, blouses, and sweaters without collars which have a tendency to ride up in a sitting position. To satisfy this preference, it is easy to remove collars and substitute bindings or inside facings as neckline finishes. In making this alteration, collars should not be merely cut off the garment, but rather the stitching should be removed in order to keep intact the seam edge which would be used in attaching a binding or facing as the new neckline finish. Facings of appropriate fabric and color, turned to the outside of the garment and finished with piping at the edge of the facings, could add to the attractiveness of the garment.

Sleeve Width Changes

For some stout women with large upper arm girth, sleeve width may need to be increased. To increase sleeve width, the sleeve should be removed from the armhole and a strip of fabric inserted in the sleeve seam to accommodate the arm girth. The fabric and color should relate to the garment fabric as well as possible in order to be inconspicuous, since it would serve a purely utilitarian purpose. When the sleeve is sewed back into the garment, the additional width should be worked in at the under arm curve of the armhole in order not to disturb the distribution of fullness in the sleeve cap. When very much width must be added to sleeves, the armseye lines may need to be lengthened to fit the larger sleeve dimensions. If additional width is not needed in the lower arm, the inset could be tapered from just below the elbow to the end of the sleeve. If additional width is needed in the lower arm, the tapering would need to start midway between the elbow and the wrist. Sleeves that are uncomfortably wide for a very slim person can be scaled down to better proportions by tapering the sleeve seams according to need. If changes also need to be made in bodice width, it would be necessary to remove the sleeves, since the armseyes would need to be recut and the sleeves made to fit the new armseyes.

Increasing and Decreasing Garment Size

If a garment is so much smaller than it needs to be that adjustments of gathers, darts, tucks, pleats, and seam allowances would not provide enough room, it would be possible to enlarge the garment by adding a section of fabric down the center front and center back or elsewhere in the garment to be consistent with the design of the garment. This could be done with fabric of contrasting color or a color repeating one of the colors in a printed fabric. The section of fabric inserted in the garment would need to be tapered to the neckline and the neckline finish would need to be adjusted accordingly. Garments can be lengthened by dropping hems and using bias facing as a finish. Bias facing material in hem width is available in many colors and in both cotton and synthetic fabrics. Another method of increasing length is to drop the hem and add a border of fabric in a contrasting color or a color that repeats one in the garment fabric. The same fabric may then be used elsewhere on the garment for trim, belt, or collar to be consistent with the design of the garment. A garment with a fitted waistline which is too short in the bodice can be easily altered to fit the taller figure by inserting fabric between the bodice and the skirt and then covering with a belt of the same fabric.

In reducing the size of a garment more than can be done with darts, gathers, tucks, pleats, and seams, it is best to take the garment apart and recut to fit the smaller size wearer. If the garment has a fitted waistline, the reduction in length should be made at both the end of the bodice and the end of the skirt to fit the figure. Garments with narrow hems can be shortened by just deepening the hems. In an alteration that involves the waistline, the closure may be involved. Zipper closures pose no problem, but button closures may come too close together after a bodice is shortened.

ALTERATION OF PATTERNS FOR MAKING CLOTHING AT HOME

Patterns for making garments for people with special needs are not available for many of the same reasons that there is so little ready-made clothing to satisfy their special needs and so few sources of specially designed and made-to-measure clothing. Therefore, standard patterns must be altered to satisfy the needs of individuals.

Dress Patterns

A pattern for a dress may have a front opening which may be needed, but the sleeves may be too long, very full, or too short, or the pattern may have no sleeves at all. In using such a pattern, sleeves could be added, short sleeves could be lengthened, or full sleeves could be altered to reduce the fullness. Alterations frequently needed to fit body contours and proportions are those for narrow shoulders, low bustline, enlarged waistline, large hips, protruding abdomen, and very stout arms.

Other alterations often needed are the deepening of armholes, provision for underlay and overlap where Velcro is to be used in place of other fastenings, change from back openings to front openings, and eliminating or adding a collar. To provide for ease in lifting the arms above the head, gussets may be added at the underarm area though they may not appear in the pattern. On belted garments, a soft tie belt, made of the garment fabric, may be substituted for a stiffened belt with a buckle and prong fastening that may be featured in the pattern. In addition to these alterations, the dimensions of garments may be altered to provide the needed extra space for various types of braces.

Sleeve and Bodice Patterns

Raglan sleeves usually allow for much more freedom of movement in the bodice of a garment than regular set-in sleeves. If more freedom of movement is needed in a garment with set-in sleeves, a simple alteration can be made in the bodice back by adding a narrow yoke at the top of the bodice, then adding the needed extra width across the back of the bodice either in gathers or pleats at the sides of the bodice back. In making this alteration, the original length of the bodice back must be retained.

Skirt Patterns

Many changes can be made in skirt patterns to adapt them to special needs. When straight skirts and dresses with straight skirts are in fashion, width can be added to the skirts by slashing the pattern at a few points from the bottom to the waistline and spreading to provide the additional width. In this alteration, the hip line coutour can be maintained while increasing the width of the garment. To maintain the original position of the side seams, the same alteration should be made on the front and the back of the skirt, unless there is need for additional width in either the front or the back. For those who use wheelchairs and those who spend much time sitting, this is a common alteration.

Fitted skirts that have a regular side or back zipper closing may be difficult for some individuals to put on. Such patterns may be changed to the wrap-around style by adding another gore or a whole front or back section to provide the needed overlay, and increasing the length of the belt accordingly. In making this alteration, the opening of the skirt may be placed where it can be most easily reached, although the pattern may show the opening placed elsewhere. Where there is a problem of finger dexterity, the band on such a skirt could be fastened with Velcro instead of a hook or button. For those who have difficulty in using any kind of fastening, the skirt band on a skirt other than wrap-style may be eliminated entirely and a hem or heading may be used at the top of the skirt for elastic. When this is done, the waistline needs to be made wide enough to fit over the shoulders or hips, which means omitting the darts and some of the fitting from hip to waistline.

Patterns for Slacks and Trousers

In addition to the lengthening of trousers and slacks to be worn by those confined to wheelchairs, the back rise should be lengthened and the front rise lowered. This calls for a simple alteration of adding a few inches to the center back and gradually tapering down to the side seams, and lowering the front rise and gradually tapering up to the side seams.

Garments Worn Over Braces

Changes can be made in some patterns to reduce the abrasion damage in garments worn over braces of various kinds. In patterns for slacks or any trouser type garments, additional width may be added at the side seams to accommodate braces. In dress patterns for girls who wear Milwaukee braces that reach up to the neck, pattern alterations may be made to provide fullness at the neckline to form a high stand-up ruffle to cover the top of the body brace. Turtle-type neckline finishing, using rib knit fabric or the garment fabric, can also be used to cover the tops of the braces that would show if collarless garments were worn.

Body Deformities

Other alterations may be made on patterns to adapt to body deformities. When one shoulder is higher than the other or one hip higher than the other, the pattern may be altered and spread to fit the higher shoulder or hip with adjustments on the side seams, maintaining the original vertical and horizontal grain lines of the pattern. Using fabrics of solid colors or printed patterns, body deformities are not as readily revealed as with plaid, checked or striped fabrics.

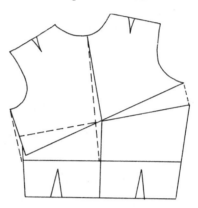

Figure 23. Pattern alteration for asymmetrical shoulders. Courtesy of the *British Journal of Occupational Therapy.*

To alter a pattern for asymmetrical shoulders, the bodice should be slashed on a line from the lower point of the armseye on the side of the higher shoulder diagonally across the bodice to the opposite side seam about half way between the lower point of the armseye and the end of the bodice. The pattern should then be spread and overlapped to conform to the shoulder levels of the figure, using the center back and center front as the point at which the spreading and overlapping begins. The side seam should be completed where the pattern was spread and a new seam line should be made to adjust to the overlapping on the opposite side of the bodice. This alteration must be made on both the back and front bodice patterns. The level of the bustline darts on the bodice front may need to be adjusted to conform to the individual figure. This alteration for asymmetrical shoulders can also be made on a one-piece dress pattern.[1]

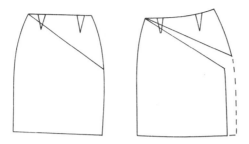

Figure 24. Pattern alteration for asymmetrical hips. Courtesy of the *British Journal of Occupational Therapy.*

To alter a skirt pattern for asymmetrical hips, the pattern should be slashed and spread from just below the higher hip diagonally to the opposite side of the skirt where the waistline meets the side seam. A new side seam on the higher hip side should be made from the upper end of the slash to the bottom of the skirt parallel to the original skirt side seam line. If there are darts at the waistline of the skirt, they should end at the same horizontal line to give the appearance of a symmetrical figure. Similar alterations should be made on other skirt styles to fit asymmetrical hips.

A curve on the upper back, about in line with the center of the armseye, is known as *kyphosis,* which requires a pattern alteration. This is an ancient term used by Hippocrates to describe a humpback, although the term was used for any bowing or curving. The term is derived from the Greek word *kyphos,* meaning humpbacked, curved, or bent, plus the suffix *osis* denoting a state of or condition of.[2] Since the curve lengthens the measurement of the back from the base of the neck to the waistline, garments such as dresses, blouses, and coats are pulled up from their normal position at the waistline and at the lower edge of the garment.

A simple alteration may be made on a pattern to fit the figure with kyphosis, which involves a seam at the center back from the neck to the waistline or, in a garment without waistline fitting, to the lower edge of the garment. The alteration is made by slashing the back bodice on a horizontal line two-thirds of

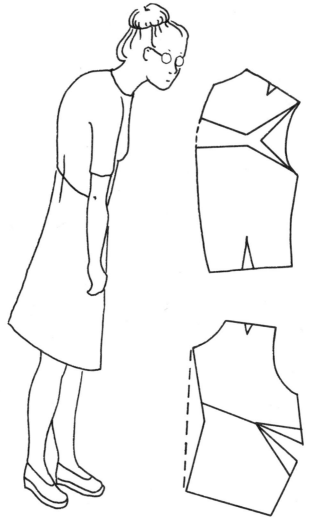

Figure 25. Pattern alteration for a curve on the upper back, known as kyphosis or hump back. Courtesy of the *British Journal of Occupational Therapy.*

the width of the bodice back pattern toward the center of the armseye curve, and then diagonally to the upper edge of the armseye and diagonally to the lower edge of the armseye, and spreading the pattern to provide the needed additional length in the back bodice. Measurement of the figure from the neckline to the waistline, compared with the pattern measurement of the length of the bodice center back, will determine how much spread will be needed to provide the additional back bodice length.[1]

The figure with kyphosis will be concave and shorter in front, and the pattern will need to be altered accordingly. The alteration is made by slashing the bodice front on a horizontal line from the center front to the tip of the bustline dart, slashing the center of the bustline dart to the tip, spreading the bustline dart and overlapping the slashed edges of the center front to shorten the bodice front as needed. A new center front line is then made by a vertical line from the neckline to the end of the bodice. In making the garment, the dart is stitched on the original dart line and the side seam of the bodice front may have to be shortened slightly to match the side seam of the bodice back.[1]

In all pattern alterations, it is important to keep the grain of the fabric in true vertical and horizontal positions in the major areas of the garment in order for the garment to hang without forming diagonal lines. Pattern alterations can easily be made by those who are knowledgeable and experienced. Detailed directions for pattern alteration may be found in most standard textbooks on clothing construction and those published by pattern companies. Occasionally, persons who assist physically handicapped and elderly persons with clothing problems, make a list of patterns in current pattern books which incorporate many desirable features and could be easily altered to satisfy other specific needs. Lists of this kind must be constantly up-dated to keep them current with changes in pattern books from which patterns are selected.

REFERENCES

1. Rogers, E. D. and Stevens, B. M.: *Dressmaking for the Disabled.* The Association for Occupational Therapists, London, England. (Reprinted from *Occupational Therapy,* Jan, Feb, March, April, and

May, 1966).
2. Wain, Harry: *The Story Behind the Word — Some Interesting Origins of Medical Terms.* Springfield, Thomas, 1958.

Chapter 7

FOOTWEAR, CLOTHING ACCESSORIES, DRESSING AND GROOMING AIDS

SATISFYING the clothing needs of the physically handicapped and the aged would not be complete without consideration of footwear, clothing accessories, and dressing and grooming aids, which contribute greatly to comfort, mobility, appearance, and psychological well-being. Involved in footwear are also the factors of protection from pain, infection, and falling, in addition to the need for accommodation to the shape and condition of the feet.

FOOTWEAR FOR THE PHYSICALLY HANDICAPPED

The greatest footwear needs of the physically handicapped are shoes that provide comfort, stability, and support, and to which braces may be attached if needed. Problems of some of the physically handicapped are not as much concerned with specific foot conditions as they are with problems of gait and balance when standing and walking. Those who cannot bend forward easily to reach their feet need shoes that are easy to put on and take off.

For shoes that lace, elastic laces may be used so that the shoes may remain laced and tied and still have enough stretch in the laces to get the shoes off and on. Buckles should be avoided for those persons who cannot easily reach their feet and also for those who lack strength and grasp necessary to fasten and unfasten buckles. To avoid the problem of manipulating buckles, it is possible to have buckles removed and a patch of Velcro added, and a new strap without holes lined with Velcro to complete the Velcro closing. This adaptation can be made by a good shoe repair man or one who is specialized in adapting shoes to meet special needs. Shoes with elasticized sides, with no fastenings at all, are easy to put on and take off for persons who cannot easily reach their feet.

Shoes for Brace Attachment

Shoes to which braces must be attached may be purchased at a regular shoe store, but they must have leather soles and steel arches, and they must be of sturdy construction. Those with plastic soles cannot be used for attaching braces, nor can very lightweight shoes of flimsy construction such as sandals, be used. Regular shoes, purchased in a shoe store, may also be used by persons with one leg shorter than the other leg of normal length. This necessitates the building up of the one shoe to compensate for the shorter leg. Cork or crepe rubber are used for this purpose in order to avoid adding excessive weight to the shoes. The upper part of the shoes above the soles remain the same.

Shoes for Mismated Feet and Amputees

Polio, injury, amputation, and disease bring about serious footwear problems. Those whose feet are not the same size must buy two pair of shoes in order to get one shoe that fits each foot, and those with a leg amputated need only one shoe instead of a pair of shoes, unless they use complete leg and foot prostheses. Not only does the cost become a burden, but also there is the problem of what to do with the left-over shoes which are too good to discard and for which it would be difficult to find someone who could use them.

An occupational therapist who was a victim of polio had the problem of different size feet; because of her own problem, she became acutely aware of the same problem confronting thousands of others in similar situations. As a result of her problem and that of so many other people, she established the National Odd Shoe Exchange in 1945, which serves as a clearinghouse and brings together those persons with mutual shoe problems so that exchange of shoes may be brought about. The Exchange does not deal with shoes, but rather with the names and addresses of persons of similar age, shoe size, and taste in shoe styles who have shoes available and who seek those with whom to exchange shoes. When persons wearing the exact opposites are discovered, such as a shoe of a given size for the right foot and a shoe for the left foot of the exact same size, they are notified and they make their own arrangements for the disposal of shoes they have and for future purchase of shoes. The National Odd Shoe Exchange was started as a free service but has now grown beyond the expectations of its founder; in order to maintain the service, a nominal membership fee is charged to those persons who make use of its service. The membership fee provides for the indexing and cross-indexing of all information needed to bring together those persons who have shoes available and those who need them.[1] Other shoe exchanges are listed in the Appendix.

FOOTWEAR FOR THE ELDERLY

Foot problems and, therefore, footwear problems are more common among the elderly than among any other segment of the population and are more common among women than among men. They are usually the result of lack of proper foot care and the wearing of ill-fitting shoes over a long period of time. Also, among the elderly, certain arteriosclerotic changes may bring about poor circulation, cold feet, numbness, and ulcers. The two medical conditions most likely to bring about foot problems are diabetes and peripheral vascular diseases; both result in slow healing, so that any skin break in the feet may lead to gangrene, which often necessitates amputation of toes, feet, or entire lower extremities.[2]

Custom-Made Shoes

It has been said that, with the exception of dental caries and the common cold, no human illness is more prevalent than foot ailments.[3] With over twenty joints in each foot and many bones, it is not surprising that arthritis is one of the most commonly cited causes for painful feet among the elderly. In those with rheumatoid arthritis, the toes undergo changes similar to those seen in the distorted fingers of arthritis victims. Feet in this condition cannot be fitted into regular shoes, and the only kind of shoes that can insure comfort and proper fit are molded shoes. First, a cast is made of each of the patient's feet in the spread, weight-bearing position, and then shoes are made from the casts. The first molded shoes, invented by Alan E. Murray in 1937, were called Space Shoes®. Since the patent is no longer in effect, many shoe manufacturers are making molded shoes; also, many other shoe manufacturers are making shoes that look like Space Shoes and are giving them special names. However, the term Space Shoes is a registered trade name which remains in effect and cannot be used by other manufacturers.[4,5]

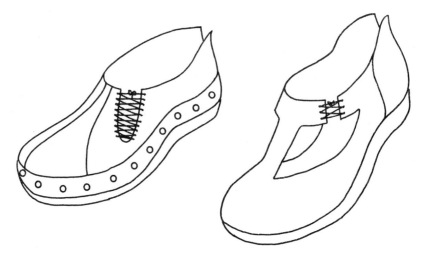

Figure 26. Space Shoes®, the first shoes made from molds of the feet for those who could not be adequately fitted with shoes manufactured in standard shapes and sizes.

Space Shoes provide comfort, protection, and accommodation to the shape of the feet, and a solution to the foot problems of many people. However, the cost is a limiting factor: including the making of the cast, it is about five times the cost of regular shoes. The first Space Shoes made were clumsy and monotonous in color, design, and general appearance, but the "second era" Space Shoes now being made have more variety in color and design, are lighter in weight, and are generally more attractive. Besides the people who have Space Shoes made in accordance with their special needs, other people who have to stand for long periods of time find that Space Shoes provide greater comfort than regular shoes. Another group of people who do not have foot problems but prefer to wear Space Shoes are tourists who do much walking as they travel.

Modifying the Shape of Shoes

For less severe foot deformities than those that require Space Shoes, regular shoes can be modified to provide special shaping for bunions and hammer toes. Shoes that need to be modified should be made of leather, both the soles and uppers, since other shoe materials do not respond to modifying processes. Also, there are some shoes made which are called "health shoes" or "corrective shoes" that fill the needs of some people. One style in these shoes laces all the way to the toes and also provides greater depth at the toes than regular shoes. Through the use of removable pads, the depth of these shoes may be changed, and lacing the shoes loosely or tightly provides another build-in adjustment.

Washable Shoes

One special footwear need of some physically handicapped and elderly persons is washable shoes that provide some stability and support. Stroke patients who are learning to walk again, other physically handicapped and elderly persons, and those with severe mental retardation often have problems of incontinence. Though they may wear moisture-proof diaper-type garments with absorbent liners, it is not unusual for leakage to occur which drains down to the feet. Leather shoes can be ruined in a short period of time, since they cannot be washed nor is there any way of getting rid of the odor of urine. Tennis shoes, with rubber soles and uppers made of canvas or a similar fabric, do not provide as much stability and support as leather shoes, but they can be laundered. Though washable shoes are a need of persons of all ages who have the problem of incontinence, the total market for such shoes is not large enough to make commercial production of washable shoes feasible. Therefore, tennis shoes remain the best solution to the problem.

Safety Factors

One of the safety hazards of elderly persons is falling, either outdoors or indoors, even in their own homes, and one of the best preventive measures is well-fitting shoes that provide the needed stability and support. While soft-soled house slippers may appear to be very comfortable, they frequently cause the wearer to fall, often resulting in broken bones, long hospitalization, and immobility. Other falling hazards are shoes that are too loose or too large.

Foot Care

While footwear is essential to health, mobility, and general well-being of the elderly, also essential is adequate foot care. Care of the feet is one of the oldest kinds of health care, dating back to centuries before the Christian era. In 1784, a book called *Chiropodologia* was published in London by David Low, which provides the origin of the word *chiropody*. The National Association of Chiropodists was organized in 1912 and by 1958 had changed its name to the American Podiatry Association. Both chiropody and podiatry are still used to mean care and treatment of foot disorders, but podiatry is the more accurate and descriptive term. Chiropody comes from the Greek word *chiro* or hand and *pod* or foot. Podiatry comes from the Greek word for foot and healing.[6] Though all medical service is costly, the advice and services of a podiatrist for the elderly, when needed, could make the difference between remaining active and mobile or moving to a nursing home.

Hosiery

Choice and use of hosiery relates to some of the problems of footwear. Either regular or support hosiery that is too tight can affect circulation, and hosiery that is too short in the foot can accentuate problems of bunions, overlapping toes, and hammer toes. In certain conditions of health, particularly diabetes, the feet are vulnerable to the slightest irritation. The irritation might not be very painful at first but could develop pressure sores that could become infected. Inside seams in the feet of hosiery could cause such irritation and also folds or wrinkles in shoe linings that have become separated from the shoes.

CLOTHING ACCESSORIES

Though most of the elderly do less dressing up and have a less active social life than younger people, their appearance, on these limited occasions, is very important in their social relationships and to their morale and psychological well-being. Choice and use of some clothing accessories are limited for the elderly because of their reduced physical strength, lack of finger dexterity, and grasp.

Jewelry

Putting jewelry on and taking it off is a part of the total dressing process and it should be just as easy to do as putting on and taking off clothing. Jewelry which hangs on the body, such as necklaces and bracelets, should not be heavy. Necklaces and bracelets made of heavy gauge metal should be discarded in favor of finer gauge metal and plastics. Bracelets that are easiest to put on and take off are those that slip over the wrists and have no fastenings or safety clasps. Even for the able-bodied, the tiny clasps at the back of short necklaces are difficult to manipulate and are more difficult for those with reduced finger dexterity. Just reaching to the back of the neck is difficult for some people. Necklaces that are long enough to put on over the head are the easiest to put on and take off.

Brooches and other pins with tiny catches or safety clasps are difficult to manage because of weak grasp and inability to move the tiny parts. Also, those persons with some sight loss may not be able to see the tiny catches and safety clasps and may think a pin is properly fastened when it is not. Only those brooches and pins with fastenings which are large enough to feel easily and to open and close easily would be useful in the jewelry collections of many older women. The easiest piece of jewelry to put on and take off is a ring, provided there are no enlarged joints on the fingers. Beside the absence of fastenings, the handling of rings does not require perfect eyesight or finger dexterity. Clip earrings are easier to put on than those that screw on, but both kinds require some finger dexterity to locate them on the ears and hold them in place.

Handbags

Handbag fashions change in size, shape, weight, color, and material. For older women, handbags should be lighter in weight and smaller in size than those carried by younger women, and not so deep that things might easily get lost from sight. Older women generally do not have as many things to carry in handbags nor do they accumulate as many things that they must carry with them. Because of the more limited number of shopping trips and other trips away from home, most older women do not need as many handbags as their younger counterparts. In terms of color and material of which the handbags are made, they should coordinate with the outer garments worn when the handbags are carried, according to the individual taste, likes, and dislikes. Fastenings on handbags should be easy to open and close, without complicated straps and buckles that take two hands to open and close or knobs that have to be inserted in holes and then turned to fasten the handbag. Some older women who use crutches prefer shoulder bags, while others prefer bags that they can manage by hand as they grasp their crutches.

Gloves

Fashions in gloves and in the wearing of gloves change, but many older women regard gloves and the wearing of gloves as a part of their culture and wear them, regardless of prevailing fashions. The best choice of gloves for older women are those that are easy to put on and take off, and cloth gloves are usually easier than leather ones even though they may not fit as snugly. Also, cloth gloves are washable and easier to keep clean than leather gloves. For very cold weather, leather gloves with wool linings provide the most warmth and are easy to put on and take off.

Umbrellas and Rainwear

Though umbrellas provide the best protection from rain, they are not suitable for either the physically handicapped nor the elderly. They require the full use of one hand and arm, and for those with a gait or balance problem, the carrying of an umbrella would add to the problem. Those who use canes, crutches, a single crutch, or any other kind of walking aid, could not manage an umbrella, nor could a person manage an umbrella who depended on a wheelchair for locomotion. The best protection from rain for both the physically handicapped and the elderly is a lightweight raincoat that sheds water. Well-styled raincoats often serve as casual all-purpose coats, thus reducing the number of coats needed while serving essential needs. All raincoats should have pockets, and raincoats with attached hoods offer the most complete protection for those who can reach the hoods and pull them up over their heads. A plastic rain bonnet of some kind should always be in the pocket of a raincoat that is not equipped with a hood. Also, a plastic rain bonnet should be carried in every handbag as protection against unexpected showers.

When pavements are wet or covered with ice or snow, it is better for the elderly and the physically handicapped to remain indoors to avoid falls which so frequently occur under such conditions. For those who must be outdoors, waterproof foot-wear should be worn. Some of the problems with such footwear are excessive weight, difficult fastenings, and the physical effort to get the footwear on and off. This is especially true of high boots which are often in fashion. Shorter plastic boots that go on over shoes, with simple fastenings, are the best choice except for those who must be outdoors for long periods of time during severe storms.

DRESSING AND GROOMING AIDS

In addition to the need for comfort, attractiveness, durability, and ease of care, clothing for the physically handicapped and the elderly must be so designed or adapted that dressing and undressing may be achieved independently and with a minimum of physical exertion. Design features that contribute to ease in dressing and undressing, and the physical conditions that affect dressing and undressing, are discussed in Chapter 5. Ability to dress and undress without assistance and to take care of grooming needs are very important for the physically handicapped and the elderly. When there is need for assistance in dressing, undressing, and grooming, the cost of care is increased: if assistance is needed and is not available, the person may not get dressed at all. Among ambulatory elderly persons in nursing homes, not being dressed in daytime clothes not only detracts from appearance but lowers the morale, adds to feelings of helplessness, and lessens the hope for recovery.

Stroke and accident victims, especially paraplegics, amputees, and brain-damaged patients, must relearn the dressing and undressing process. The relearning involves detailed analysis of motion and adaptation of methods to suit the specific condition of the individual. Factors in the analysis of motion include extent, location, and degree of limitations; ability to grasp and manipulate; hand dexterity, sitting balance in a chair, wheelchair, or on a bed; and ability to raise the arms above the head.

Dressing Aids

Many mechanical aids and other devices are available for use in the dressing process but they are not stocked in clothing stores or in department stores. Most of them are available only through special mail order catalogs which feature self-help devices for independent living and equipment for physical medicine. A list of catalogs appears in the Appendix.

Devices that appear in many of the catalogs include button-hooks for buttoning small buttons such as those on the front of men's shirts, clamps for holding garments in place while dressing with one hand, and tongs for reaching things too far away to reach by hand. Also available are elastic shoe laces so that shoes may be laced and tied permanently. Elastic laces provide enough stretch to get shoes on and off easily. Devices for use in putting shoes on easily include a long-handled shoe-horn which is especially helpful for those who cannot reach their feet, and a device for positioning shoes so that they do not move in the process of getting the feet into them.

With limited range of motion and hand function, zippers can be difficult to manage. For zipper closures in shoes, a dowel stick with a hook at the end is helpful: when such a device is used, a ring should be attached to the zipper pull to make it easier to insert the hook at the end of the dowel stick.

For those who have difficulty in putting on hosiery, a useful device is a circular band which is inserted in the sock or stocking with cords attached to the sides so that the foot can slip in and pulling motion can get the sock or stocking completely on. However, since this device sometimes causes runs in socks and stockings, it is best used with mesh or other run-proof construction. This device is not suitable for use with support hosiery because the stretch factor makes it difficult to pull them on.[7, 8]

Putting on neckties, either the bow or knotted type, is difficult or impossible for some men with limited range of motion and limited hand function. One device which eliminates the problem is a narrow round plastic clip open in the back, that goes around the neck under the shirt collar, to which the tied or knotted tie is permanently attached. The clip, which can be put on with one hand, does not show when the shirt collar is turned down.

Care and Storage of Clothing

One constant problem in the care of clothing is the removal of stains from food that drops on clothing. One way to minimize this problem is to treat outer garments with stain repellents. To remove lint that collects on some outer garments, a small plastic roller covered with adhesive tape removes lint more easily than brushing and may be easier to handle than a brush.

Care of shoes can be difficult for those with limited reach and hand function. For polishing, individual shoe shine pads can be used which are discarded after one use, and spray polish is also available. Another means of polishing that may be easier for some people to use is a battery powered or electric polisher that requires no bending over and can be used in either a sitting or standing position.

Some simple changes can be made to increase the convenience and efficiency of storage of clothing in closets. For wheelchair users, regular closet doors can be removed and replaced with folding doors or curtains on large rings that move easily. Rods for hanging clothes can be installed at a lower level in order to reach clothes more easily and also a reaching stick can be used to lift hangers from the rods. For greater ease in removing clothes from rods, nylon hanger guides can be used to space garments so that individual garments can be seen at a glance. Garments that slip off wire hangers and fall to the floor are a nuisance in any closet and one way to avoid having garments slip off hangers is to use hangers covered with cloth or a thin layer of foam. Shelves in most closets are high and are difficult for many people to reach. To make shelf space more useful, shelves can be lowered so that they can be reached more easily. Also, chest drawers should be low enough to reach from a sitting position.

Shoe storage poses a problem when there is no choice but a high shelf or the floor. For those who have a problem in moving about and in reaching, the best shoe storage is a shoe rack on rollers which can be easily reached and moved. In addition to closets, bureau drawers provide the largest area of storage space in bedrooms, but often bureau drawers get stuck, especially when pulled open with one hand instead of two. For easier action and for one hand manipulation, bureau drawers should be mounted on ball bearings or nylon glides. Also a drawer pull attached to the center of the drawer makes it easier for one-handed manipulation.

Grooming Aids

One essential piece of equipment used by all people in the process of grooming is a mirror, and for those who do not have access to mirrors in their usual locations or cannot hold mirrors in their hands, there are some mirrors especially designed for them. For bed patients, there are mirrors that can be attached to the head of the bed on an extension arm, and also mirrors that can be attached to lap boards. Other types of mirrors are those that are attached to cords or chains that go around the neck with adjustable positioning of the mirrors, and mirrors on extension arms attached to walls set at convenient levels for use.

Care of the hair is important to most people and there are some devices that are helpful. There are combs and brushes mounted on extension handles that can be used by those with limited reach, and for those with enough reach but a weak grip, there is a brush with a loop on the back that slips over the hand to position the brush for action. There are also battery operated brushes and electric brushes. For individuals who have no use of hands or arms, combs can be mounted in such a position that neck action can be used to comb the hair.

For application of cosmetics, extension handles can also be used for those with limited reach, and some spray-type cosmetics simplify the process. Also, for those with limited reach, there are nose blowers complete with tissue holders. Shaving is a problem for men who have a limited range of motion and hand function. To make it possible for them to shave independently, razors can be mounted on extension handles and shaving brushes can be held in extension clamps. When there is sufficient range of motion but weak grasp, razors can be attached to the fingers or the hand by means of a loop much the same as a hair brush. Cordless battery operated razors or electric razors increase safety, reduce stress, and eliminate the handling of blades.

Some very simple devices can be used in the care of the fingernails. A brush for cleaning the nails can be attached to a smooth surface by suction and a file can also be stabilized so that the fingernails can move over the file instead of the file moving over the nails. A nail clipper can be adapted from a stapler and there is also a battery powered filing device available.[7, 8]

REFERENCES

1. National Shoe Exchange, Santa Monica, California.
2. Tarara, Edward L.: *Podiatry's Role in the Care of the Aged.* Paper presented at Annual Meeting of the American Podiatry Association, Chicago, August 1960.
3. Root, Lin: Getting the most out of your feet. *Today's Health, 39*(2):50-51, 65-66, March, 1961.
4. Dixon, A. S.: Space shoes in rheumatoid arthritis. *Physiotherapy, 53*(4):141, April, 1967.
5. Murray, Alan E.: Personal communication, September 28, 1974.
6. Various Ailments of the Feet Are Common Among the People of the U. S. *Journal of the National Association of Retail Druggists, LXXXII* (23):6-7, 62.
7. Klinger, Judith: *Self-Help for Arthritic Patients.* Allied Health Professions Section, The Arthritis Foundation, 1974.
8. Lowman, Edward W. and Rusk, Howard A.: *Self-Help Devices.* Rehabilitation Monograph XXI, Institute of Rehabilitation, New York University Medical Center, 1967.

Chapter 8

CLOTHING NEEDS RELATED TO OTHER PHYSICAL CONDITIONS

PHYSICAL conditions which bring about special clothing needs, in addition to those already considered, include effects of breast surgery, incontinence and the use of ileal conduits and colostomies, severe burns, epilepsy, visual impairment, and problems of weight and stature.

EFFECTS OF BREAST SURGERY

Cancer of the breast necessitates the surgical removal of the breast or part of the breast by an operation known as a mastectomy. Though exact figures on the incidence of breast cancer are not available, it was estimated by the American Cancer Society in 1974 that there were 90,000 new cases of breast cancer and that 33,000 women died from breast cancer that year. It was also estimated that one out of every fifteen girls born during the year will have breast cancer later in life. In relation to the rate of population growth, it was noted that the incidence of breast cancer is increasing faster than the rate of population growth.[1]

Breast cancer is not of recent origin. The ancient Egyptians made observations about breast lumps or swellings, and the first recorded incidence of surgical breast removal dates back to 520 BC, and about 400 BC, Hippocrates mentioned breast cancer.[2] In the first century, it was reported that breast amputations were performed but the procedure fell into disuse and was then revived in the sixteenth century. The term *mastectomy* is composed of the Greek words *mastos* or breast and *ektome* or excision.[3] Mastectomy operations are classified on the basis of their severity. The most severe is called the *radical* or *total* mastectomy in which not only the entire breast is removed, but also the chest wall muscles, underarm lymph nodes, and associated tissues. A less severe operation is called the *modified*

125

radical in which the breast and the lymph nodes are removed but not the chest muscles. The *simple* mastectomy removes only the breast when the tumor has not effected the nodes, and the *partial mastectomy* removes only the tumor and a part of the breast.

Physical Effects of Mastectomy Operations

After a mastectomy operation, the arm may swell because the lymph nodes and vessels were removed and the body becomes less able to combat infection in the extremities. Treatment consists of antibiotic therapy to control infection and the use of an elastic sleeve and a separate elastic gauntlet to minimize the swelling in the upper arm, forearm, and hand, which is known as lymphedema. As the swelling is reduced, new measurements are taken for a smaller size elastic sleeve so that maximum pressure is applied at all times. A sense of physical loss and permanent change in appearance requires much emotional adjustment. Postmastectomy lymphedema usually occurs within a year but may occur some years later, may be very distressing and often disabling, and may cause psychological suffering in addition to pain, extra weight, and loss of function.[4] The swelling of the arm limits the design of sleeves that can be worn, and fluctuation in the swelling necessitates design changes and enlargements in armholes and in sleeves of garments to allow them to hang and drape gracefully on the figure.

Another effect of a mastectomy operation, depending on the severity of the operation, is the off-balance sensation due to the loss of weight on one side. To compensate for the loss of weight and the loss of body contour, prosthetic devices, called breast forms, are used which visually replace the missing breast contour. Materials used for breast forms are foam, air-inflated plastic, air-and-fluid-filled plastic, liquid-filled plastic, weighted and unweighted rubber, and silicone-gel-filled rubber. Foam is lightweight and does not provide for the loss of weight, especially in large breast sizes. Silicone most closely approximates weight of the normal breast. Weighting material of various kinds can be added to some breast forms.[2]

Clothing Needs and Availability

In addition to breast forms, specially designed postmastectomy bras with pockets for the breast forms are also necessary. Both breast forms and bras with pockets for breast forms are made by many manufacturers in a wide range of prices and a variety of styles and fabrics, which are sold in specialty stores and department stores, by corsetieres and surgical supply dealers, national chain stores, and catalog stores. In New York, there is a boutique shop exclusively for women who have had mastectomy operations, specializing in apparel, accessories, and other needs of mastectomy patients. Also, there are custom-made breast forms, which the makers claim to be exact duplicates of the remaining breast, and there are "made to measure" bras available from some sources. In stores where postmastectomy bras are sold, it has been found that the sales people who do the best fitting are those who have had mastectomy operations themselves.

Choice of bras should be made according to the extent of the surgery and the fullness of the bust. One important function of the postmastectomy bra is to hold the breast form in place to approximate a normal appearance. Two important features in postmastectomy bras are built-up shoulder areas to compensate for the lost muscle tissue, and shoulder strap control achieved by fastening a connecting strap across the upper back to avoid scar irritations.

Following the radical mastectomy operation, there are hollow places in the upper breast areas from removal of the pectoral muscle, and pads are often used to fill in under the built-up bra. Wide shoulder straps generally provide greater comfort than narrow ones and sometimes shoulder pads are used. In bras which have metal adjustments in the front section of the shoulder straps for lengthening or shortening the straps, it may be necessary to shift the metal pieces to avoid touching the areas involved in the surgery. Sometimes, there is need to adjust the bra pockets to achieve a better fit for breast forms. Pockets should be adjusted and forms inserted so that the lower edge of the breast form is at the same level as the other breast.[2]

One line of apparel specially designed by some manufacturers for women who have had mastectomy operations is swim wear. Features of the specially designed swim wear are higher necklines, high and tight armholes to cover scars, and built up backs and fronts with front zipper closings. The special needs are to cover the affected areas including front and back and under arms, depending on the type of surgery performed and the degree of scarring. In addition to the "covered up" styles, another way to cover up scars, blemishes, or discoloration of the skin is to use an opaque cream which comes in ten colors and may be blended to match the skin tone.

Reach to Recovery Program

The REACH TO RECOVERY program was started by Terese Lasser, who had breast cancer surgery in 1952 and suffered the overwhelming anxieties so many women experience. Mrs. Lasser longed to have someone to talk with who had the same surgery experience, and who could give counsel, reassurance, and understanding, but she had to find out by trial and error how to cope with all the problems of dress and wardrobe adjustments following breast surgery, including the selection of breast prostheses or breast forms. However, it was when a friend suggested to her that she visit a mutual friend who was then hospitalized following breast surgery that the idea for REACH TO RECOVERY was born. For the first few years she worked alone, and she then recruited volunteers, who had recovered from breast surgery. At this time, over 6500 volunteers have been trained to participate in the program and are now helping new patients through the traumatic experience in more than 2500 hospitals in the United States. In 1969, the program was merged with the American Cancer Society and Terese Lasser became the National Coordinator and Consultant.[2]

REACH TO RECOVERY is a free service and is not an organization. This service is available, with the attending physician's approval, to any woman who has had breast cancer surgery. The volunteer, who is trained to give this service, calls on the patient in the hospital and, in addition to talking with the patient, assures her that her femininity will not be affected by the surgery. The volunteer brings, for the patient, a breast form for temporary use in approximately the right size which can be pinned into a bra when she leaves the hospital. After adequate healing, the physician tells the patient when she is ready to select and wear a permanent breast form. During the volunteer's visit with the patient, she discusses the various kinds of breast forms and special bras available and gives the patient a list of the breast forms and bras available which includes brand names, descriptions, where available, and approximate prices. Other items on the lists are lounging and sleeping bras and cosmetics to cover scars and other effects of surgery. Another list gives sources of specially designed swim wear. The lists are comprehensive and are revised yearly by Terese Lasser, who keeps up to date on market offerings.[2]

The volunteer also gives the patient a copy of the fifty page *Reach to Recovery* manual, written by Terese Lasser, which includes coping with psychological effects of the surgery, clothing adjustments, information on breast forms and bra needs, and exercises to strengthen muscles. The manual has been translated into many languages and is now in use around the world.

INCONTINENCE AND URINARY AND FECAL DIVERSIONS

The loss of voluntary control of elimination of urine and feces from the body is defined as incontinence. This condition affects many people and makes certain clothing adaptations necessary. Incontinence is present in children with neuromuscular conditions, severe spina bifida, and other physical conditions and is also present in adolescents and adults with neuromuscular conditions such as paraplegia and quadraplegia and other problems that affect muscle control. This condition is especially prevalent among older patients in nursing homes. There is no estimate of the number of people who have problems of incontinence since this is not a reportable health condition.

When the normal function of the bladder or bowels is lost, it is necessary to provide other means of elimination by which the urine and feces are diverted from the normal pathway. A urinary diversion is any type of operative procedure which diverts the flow of urine from the normal pathway. An example of a urinary diversion is the *ileal conduit* diversion or the passage of the urine from the kidney, by way of the ureter, to the surface of the body. The ileal conduit is actually a piece of the bowel which has been separated from the normal pathway of the intestines and delivers the urine from the urinary tract to the surface of the body; a *urether* is the tubular structure which normally joins the kidneys to the bladder.[5]

In order to understand the process of diversion, it is necessary to define more of the terms in the urological vocabulary. The word *ostomy* is a suffix which means an opening somewhere on the surface of the abdomen. Examples of ostomies are a *colostomy* (fecal diversion), which is the opening of the bowel onto the surface of the body, and a *ureterostomy* (urinary diversion), which is the opening of a ureter to the surface of the body. The *stoma* is defined as the place where the segment of the bowel or the ureter joins the surface of the body. The term *appliance* is used to refer to the plastic or rubber bag which collects the feces or urine. Such an appliance has a flat, disclike surface and is usually round or oval in shape.[5]

Diversion operations are performed where disease-oriented or neuromuscular conditions interfere with the normal functioning of the bladder and bowels. In young children, the need for such diversions may be the result of a defect in the urinary tract which causes the urine to back up into the kidneys; among some adults, diversion operations are performed on those who are incontinent and want to do away with the need for frequent changes of liners in waterproof garments and avoid the embarrassment of leakage from waterproof garments. Patients who have diversionary operations are carefully instructed by doctors and nurses in the case of the skin around the stoma and the attachment of the appliance to avoid infection, leakage, and odor. The stoma is located on the flattest part of the abdomen and the drainage bag or appliance is attached to the skin around the stoma.

People who have various physical handicaps have organizations for the purpose of exchange of helpful information and moral support, and there are many "ostomy" clubs. Those who have had diversionary operations are called *ostimates* and there are over 1 million in the United States. There are over 55,000 new surgeries performed each year and in 1977, there were 458 ostomy clubs with a total of 31,800 members. One important service which the ostomy clubs perform is to visit in hospitals with patients who are about to have diversionary operations, to relieve them of anxiety they may feel about the probable outcome of the operations and the effect on their daily lives, including clothing adaptations.[6]

In some older adults, momentary loss of muscle control is sometimes caused by laughing, coughing, and sneezing, and in others, there is constant drainage. For women who experience spasmodic leakage brought on by laughing, coughing, and sneezing, sanitary napkins, as used for menstruation, may take care of their needs. When spasmodic or continual drainage occurs, waterproof trunks or panties with absorbent liners solve the problem. These special waterproof garments and liners are available from hospital supply sources and also from the mail order catalogs of the chain department stores. The liners are washable and can be reused.

Clothing Adaptations

The need for clothing adaptations depends somewhat on how bulky the appliances are and how much they show in the silhouette of the body. Men who wear drainage bags in the abdominal area may find it difficult to wear belts on their trousers and may find it more convenient to wear suspenders. When drainage bags attached to a catheter are used, additional width in trouser legs and lower leg zippers add comfort and convenience in handling drainage bags. Worn in the abdominal area, drainage bags also limit the use of some garments for women. A girdle cannot be worn unless there is a hole cut in the girdle to accommodate the stoma area and the bag. Also, no tight garments should be worn around the abdominal area from the waist to the pelvic bone. Skirts should be A-line, gored, gathered or pleated rather than straight without any fullness. Slacks should fit in the abdominal area and may be made with an elasticized waist or a narrow fitted waist with fullness in the form of small pleats, tucks, or gathers below the band.

For those troubled with incontinence who are unable to care for themselves and require assistance, easily managed outergarments make changes easier and less time-consuming. For women, wrap-type or back-opening slips, skirts, and dresses are easier to manage than those with front or side openings or which must be taken off. Those who experience occasional leakage and soiling of outer garments find it advantageous to wear two-piece garments such as tops and slacks or skirts so that only the lower piece needs to be changed, rather than the whole one-piece dress.

EPILEPSY

A *seizure* may be defined as a sudden or violent involuntary muscular contraction in which the victim loses balance and falls. *Convulsion* is another term to identify seizure activity. This word is derived from the Latin word meaning plucked or torn away. This term is an ancient one, known to have been used in the first century. Convulsive diseases have been known since antiquity and one which is identified by name is *epilepsy*. This has been called by many different names at different times and it was suspiciously believed that the disease was a punishment for offending the gods, especially visited upon those who sinned against the moon. The Greek origin of the word meant a seizure. Thus, the term epilepsy literally meant that the victim was seized upon and taken by the gods. The disease was also called *falling sickness.*[3]

Though there are no exact causes for seizures, it is believed that they may be caused by many conditions including endocrine imbalance, certain brain conditions, other physical abnormalities, and conditions of genetic origin. There is no exact count of the number of people who have epilepsy, and estimates range from 2 to 6 million. A conservative estimate is that about 2 million Americans have epilepsy and that, of this number, about 150,000 have multiple handicaps such as cerebral palsy and mental retardation; of those, about 70,000 are in institutions. The Epilepsy Foundation of America estimates that there are 4 million who have epilepsy.[7]

Epileptic seizures are generally classified as (1) grand mal, (2) petit mal, and (3) psychomotor. The grand mal type is the most frequent and is characterized by loss of consciousness and falling to the ground and is followed by convulsive movements of the body. After the seizure, which lasts only a minute or two, the victim is generally confused and drowsy and may sleep for several hours. Grand mal seizures can occur one or more times daily or less frequently. The petit mal type, which occurs most commonly in children, consists of a momentary blackout, of less than a minute in duration, but may occur many times in an hour. It is characterized by staring and rhythmic blinking of the eyes or other small twitching movements and lapses of consciousness, but the victim is seldom aware that he has had a seizure and resumes activity as if nothing had happened. The psychomotor type may occur at any age and may take a variety of forms such as chewing, lip smacking, confusion, dizziness, buzzing or ringing in the ears, and strong emotions such as fear or rage. A seizure may last from several minutes to hours, and following the attack, the victim is unable to remember what happened.[8]

One of the greatest hazards in falling is the likelihood of causing severe injury to the head, chin, mouth and teeth, eyes, and nose; another is that of falling against a space heater or other source of fire which could easily ignite clothing and result in severe burn injury. The best precaution to avoid the danger of injury from burns is for the seizure-prone person to wear outer garments that are nonflammable. Those subject to frequent seizures should also wear some kind of adequate head protection to avoid serious injury from falls. In addition to victims of epilepsy, those who have the ataxia form of cerebral palsy need head protection because of falls caused by poor balance and shaking of the body which interfere with control of body motion.

Protective Headgear

Protective headgear is included in the general category of special clothing needs because it can be made of polyetheylene foam covered with fabric which can be fastened with Velcro, so the fabric covering may be easily removed for laundering. This kind of protective helmet is made by the people who make special clothing items for the physically handicapped and is included in catalogs of clothing, aids, and accessories. Other sources of protective headgear are sports equipment suppliers. However, most of the protective helmets used by hockey, la crosse, and football players are not well adapted to the needs of seizure victims because of their weight and lack of ventilation. The major requirements are adequate protection, impact resistance, and shock absorbency without excessive weight. Helmets for seizure victims must also fit well, be comfortable, and provide for adequate ventilation.

Appearance is also a major factor in the selection and use of

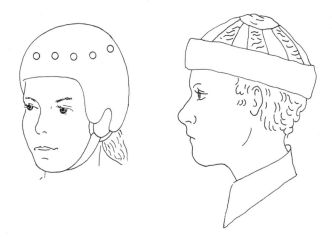

Figure 27. Protective headgear or helmets for epilepsy victims to avoid head injuries caused by falling.

protective helmets. The question arises as to how much protection can be sacrificed for acceptable appearance, especially when facial protection is needed. Some helmets are equipped with chin guards, some with chin guards and partial face guards, and others with complete face guards. Research pertinent to the development of adequate protective headgear is currently being conducted in the Division of Rehabilitation Medicine at the George Washington University Medical Center in Washington, D.C. In this research, a material with high shock absorbency is being used which was developed by the National Aeronautics and Space Administration. This is being used in a kind of head covering made over a mold of the patient's head. One other development of significance in the field of protective headgear is the work of the National Bureau of Standards in establishing standards of head protection for persons with epilepsy and related disorders, and in the testing of prototypes.[9]

BURNS

The major causes of burns are fuels, flames, scalds, and electricity: The fuels are flammable liquids; the sources of flames are matches, open space heaters, kitchen ranges, outdoor fires, and gas water heaters; scalds come from hot water, vaporizers, and hot food and drinks; the sources of electrical burns are wall sockets, extension cords, defective wiring, and power lines.

Each year, in the United States, about 80,000 people are hospitalized for treatment of burns, and of this number, about 12,000 die. The problem of burns has become known as the "silent epidemic." Most burns occur in and around the home, particularly the kitchen, utility room, garage and yard, and those at highest risk for burns are the young, the aged, and the mentally retarded and physically infirm. Many of these individuals have neither the physical capability nor the presence of mind to protect themselves from scalding liquids or to extinguish or remove burning clothing. When clothing burns, an injury of lethal degree can easily occur in one minute.

Many who treat burns believe that the next important advance in this field will be in prevention. In the United States, recent federal legislation requires that flame retardant fabric be used in the manufacture of night wear in sizes for children. Although this is an important advance, it is clearly not enough. People in high risk groups, including the institutionalized and those with seizure disorders, also deserve to be protected with flame retardant clothing.[10]

Burns are classified according to the severity with the least severe called first degree burns or superficial burns which leave no permanent scars and cause only temporary discoloration. Second degree or deep partial burns are those which cause the greatest problems in that they leave conspicuous scars after healing. Third degree or full burns are those which require skin grafts.

Pressure Dressings and Supports

While the burned skin is maturing, the burned area of the body is wrapped in pressure dressings for protection, to assist circulation, and to control scarring. Generally, pressure dressings are rolled elastic bandages, tubular elastic stockinette, and plastic stockings. They are used from six months to a year while the burns are maturing and must be changed daily. They are washable and are used again as long as they are needed. After healing, pressure bandages keep scars from raising up on the surface of the body and from contracting across joints (which would cause loss of normal functioning) and help to maintain body contours.

Some areas of the body are difficult to wrap in pressure dressings to maintain normal contours during the healing process. For these areas, special supports are used which are custom-made by the Jobst Institute of Toledo, Ohio, and are called pressure gradient garments since they provide regulated pressure. Jobst garments are made of a specially designed material with yarn made of a rubber core, wrapped in cotton, and then woven with Dacron®. This is a thin, yet very strong type of material which is 60 percent porous and therefore allows good aeration and cooling. Jobst burn supports are used for the face and head, upper chest, torso, hands, arms, and legs.

Jobst burn supports and Jobst garments are ordered by hospital medical personnel and made to measure for the individual patient, so they are quite expensive; since they need to be changed daily and washed, it is necessary to have two instead of only one. These supports and garments are worn from six months to a year, depending on the severity of the burns. In children, during this period of time, there are likely to be changes in height and weight, which necessitates the making of supports and garments to new measurements. In adults, while there is no general growth factor, there may be an increase in weight and also some edema which could necessitate the making of supports and garments to new measurements.[11]

Clothing

After the patient is discharged from the hospital, the clothing that the patient will wear must be given some consideration. Scars often cause contraction of the skin and loss of flexibility which could make reaching and handling of fastenings on clothing difficult. Generally, garments with front closings are easier to manage than those with back or side closings. Electrical and other deep burns on the hands may result in amputations of fingers or whole hands or loss of function. Victims of such severe burns are later fitted with prostheses that provide limited ability to handle clothing and fastenings. Zippers, Velcro, and elasticized areas are usually easiest to manage for those fitted with prostheses that take over the hand functions.

In cases of severe burns where much of the body is affected, clothing should be easy to put on and take off in order to encourage the patient to become independent in dressing and undressing, and to use elbows, wrists, and shoulders in order to avoid the loss of function that could result from lack of use. Clothing should be so designed as to permit freedom of motion for exercises that the patient must do in order to maintain flexibility and decrease the possibility of contractures. It is important for the patient to become responsible for all A D L (activities of daily living) and clothing should contribute to this rather than be a hindrance. Clothing should contribute to comfort, and when worn over pressure dressings and splints, it might be necessary to use garments in a larger size.

Clothing worn over scars must not be tight because the slightest pressure could cause discomfort and pain. According to the severity of burns, it takes from a month to a year to regain normal feeling and to withstand the normal pressure of clothing. Men with severe burns in the waist area or the torso would be more comfortable wearing suspenders on trousers rather than belts. Clothing worn over scars or skin grafts needs to be free of irritating elements such as bulky seams, harsh fabrics, and scratchy surfaces that could cause pressure, friction, or itching.

In case of burns on the arms and legs, it is sometimes necessary to hold the arms and legs in an outstretched position to avoid contractures, and with severe burns in the neck area, it is necessary to hold the head erect. For purposes of maintaining these positions, plastic splints are used over or under the pressure dressings. Splints on the arms and legs are usually used only at night but they may be used at other times also according to need. Neck splints, however, are kept in place during the day as well as at night. This sometimes makes it necessary to use larger size garments and those with larger neck openings if they are put on over the head.[11]

Upon leaving the hospital, members of the family of the patient are given instructions in the handling of the pressure dressings and in the appropriate use of clothing. The major effort is to return the patient to normal functioning and to keep scars to a minimum.

VISUAL IMPAIRMENT

People who are blind or who have visual impairments of some degree are usually referred to as visually handicapped. Those who are visually handicapped have clothing problems of a very different nature from those who are physically handicapped. They have virtually no clothing needs in terms of special design or fabric. Instead, their problems relate to shopping for clothes, identifying garments in their own wardrobes, storing their clothes and caring for them. There are gradations of visual impairment in addition to total blindness and each imposes certain limitations. Those, who have some vision are generally called partially sighted and they include travel vision, legally blind, and educationally blind. Travel vision means enough vision to use public transportation but not enough to drive a car. Those called legally blind do not have enough vision for employment that requires normal vision, and those called educationally blind do not have enough vision to read print of the size found in most books. They can, however, read large print which is provided especially for them.

Shopping for Clothes

In shopping for clothes, the blind or otherwise visually impaired persons must rely on information about color, design, and fabric provided by salespeople or a friend or family member whose judgment they trust who accompanies them on their shopping trips. Fiber content and care instructions on garment labels must be read to them, but they can get a good mental picture of a garment by feeling the various areas such as the neckline, openings, sleeve ends, pockets, belts, gathers, and pleats. As fashion changes occur, they must be told about them so they will know what to expect and accept since being in fashion is important to those who are blind or otherwise visually impaired. Garments which are prepackaged and cannot be tried on or even felt by hand present a problem, but the same types of garments are usually available from open stock, which would be advantageous for those dependent on feeling rather than seeing.[12]

Garment Identification and Storage

Garments in a wardrobe can be identified by feeling and fabric texture, but color identification is also important in order that all garments worn at one time will be harmonious in color. This can be achieved through the use of braille, which is a system of notation used by the blind and read by the fingers, which employs some sixty combinations of raised dots. The idea for this system was credited to Charles Barbier in 1820. However, it remained for Louis Braille, a blind teacher of the blind to introduce and popularize the system in Paris in about 1829. While Braille gave credit to Barbier for the idea, the system was named in honor of Braille. For those who learned braille, there is a method of color-coding garments by means of sewing a small thin metal wafer to the inside back of the neckline, where labels usually appear, on which the color of the garment is noted in braille. On slacks, trousers, and skirts, the wafer is sewed to the inside back of the waistband. By arranging the dots in various combinations, sixty-three different dot patterns are possible, and it is some of these dot patterns that represent each of the letters of the alphabet and punctuation marks. Braille is read by moving the hand or hands from left to right along each line and is usually done with the index finger but the middle and ring fingers can also be used.[12,13]

Some people who lose their eyesight later in life and do not learn braille must depend on another type of color identification that can be felt like braille. One effective substitute for braille is French knots made with coarse embroidery thread on a small piece of fabric which is sewed to the inside back of the neckline of the garment or the inside back of the waistline. Feeling and memory become more acute in visually handicapped persons than in sighted persons and serves as a means of identifying specific garments in the individual wardrobe.

In storing clothing in closets and chest drawers, arrangement can make it easy to identify specific items of clothing. Dividers can be used on racks where garments are hung and dividers can be used in drawers for undergarments and other clothing items. For small accessories, such as jewelry, plastic trays with compartments of different sizes are useful. Arrangement of clothing in closets and drawers and smaller items in trays is readily learned and memorized, which facilitates the use of clothing for everyday wear and for special occasions. When in doubt, the color, design, and texture can "be read" with the fingers. Arrangement of shoes on a rack can also be memorized and the hands can verify the memory.[12]

PROBLEMS OF WEIGHT AND STATURE

People who are very much overweight, much taller than average height, or much shorter than average height have difficulty in finding clothing on the ready-to-wear market that fits their unusual body proportions. The first problem recognized by manufacturers of clothing and by stores where clothing is sold was that of the overweight customer who needed clothing larger than the standard sizes made by most manufacturers; within the first decade of this century, clothing made especially for stout women appeared on the market. Though there are no statistics on the number of overweight people in the population, the various estimates that have been made suggests that there is a sizable market for clothing for overweight people. The store that first featured clothing for stout women was also the first to feature maternity wear earlier in the same decade. Later came half sizes for short waisted women, and by midcentury, clothing for chubby girls, tall women, and a few years later, clothes for chubby teenagers and short women also appeared. Soon after the appearance of the larger sizes in clothing, shoes in larger sizes also appeared on the market and in mail order catalogs.

Much clothing in the unusual sizes appears in a number of mail order catalogs, but stores that sell the unusual sizes are still not easily accessible to all the people in need. Most of the stores are located in major cities and other high population areas. Thus, many people who require unusual sizes and cannot get to the stores and those who do not want to order from mail order catalogs must either make their clothing themselves or have it made for them by family members or local dressmakers. In most large cities, there are some tailors who specialize in making clothing for people of unusual weight and stature. Sources of special size clothing appear in the Appendix.

Overweight

Those who deviate very much from average weight and girth are conspicuous, and extreme overweight is considered to be socially unacceptable by some people. Many extremely overweight people are looked upon as being repulsive and are socially abandoned, which reduces their feeling of belongingness and personal worth and adds to their problems of personal identity. Any person who deviates very much from average body size and proportions is likely to be stared at and the viewer usually makes negative judgment of the person on the basis of unusual appearance. Therefore, clothing for the overweight person becomes very important, so that regardless of the size and body proportions, the person can make an attractive appearance. The terms *overweight* and *obese* are generally used to describe a person who deviates from normal size for age and height. *Obese* literally means to overeat. It is derived from the Latin word *ob,* meaning up or over, and *edo,* meaning to eat.[3] Those who are 20 percent overweight for age and height are said to be obese.

In selecting patterns and determining the alterations to be made, the special needs of the individual overweight woman must be considered. Body contour lines, particularly shoulder and waistlines, may be quite indistinct so that patterns with raglan sleeves, rather than set-in sleeves, may fit better and look better. In using set-in sleeves, especially with sloping shoulders, it is difficult to locate armseye lines so that the silhouette does not appear distorted. Also, raglan sleeves do not reveal the girth of the upper arms as clearly as do set-in sleeves.

In most overweight figures, the waistline is much larger than in normal weight figures, and patterns with fitted waistlines tend to accentuate the large waistline. Therefore, patterns that do not have fitted waistlines or much other waistline shaping are usually a better choice for the very overweight figure. In order to not draw attention to the waistline area, it is better to eliminate belts of any kind even though they may be included in the pattern adapted for the overweight figure. In most large, overweight figures, not only is there no clearly defined waistline but, also, the abdomen protrudes; the use of belts or shaping at the waistline accentuates the protruding abdomen.

Some stout figures are "barrel"-shaped while others may be especially stout only in the shoulder and bodice area or only in the hip area so that waistline fitting could be retained and would not detract from the silhouette. Some bustline fitting is necessary and may need to be raised or lowered according to the individual figure. Good fitting adds to the feeling and appearance of being attractive and well dressed, and for the overweight woman, it is especially important.

Dresses that open all the way down the front are suggested for women who have a limited range of arm motion and cannot raise their arms above their heads, but for the very overweight, dresses that are put on over the head are better than those that button down the front or are fastened with a separating zipper. On a large figure, gapping often occurs between buttons and it may be difficult for a very large person to reach down to the lower buttons or to the bottom of a separating zipper. Neckline finishes must also be selected with care. Many overweight women tend to have short necks, so flat neckline finishes are better than standing collars. Faced necklines and sewn down collars that give the appearance of regular collars are more pleasing and do not accentuate the shortness of the neck and the girth of the figure in the neck area.

Some overweight women are taller than average and some are shorter. For those who are shorter, both ready-made garments and patterns, called "half-sizes," are available which are proportioned for women who are short. Both garments and patterns are approximately one inch shorter in the bodice and one inch shorter in the skirt and are also a bit larger in the waistline than misses and women's patterns of comparable size. All the major pattern companies provide a line of half-size patterns, and in ready-made garments, half-sizes are sold at most of the clothing stores and department stores and through mail order catalogs.

Tall Stature

Population statistics do not include stature details, but judging from the ready-to-wear market for both women and men, as a response to demand, there is an increasing proportion of tall people in the population. One chain of women's clothing stores, founded in 1900, which deals exclusively with special size categories of clothing, featured half-sizes about twenty years before talls. Before the market became responsive to the clothing needs of tall people, clothing either had to be made by those in need or made for them by dressmakers and tailors. The only other alternative for women was to purchase the best size available and then make alterations such as letting out hems and facing the ends of dresses, skirts, and coats, but lengthening the sleeves of garments and bodices of dresses was difficult or impossible. Tall sizes are generally proportioned for those five feet seven to eleven inches; some stores offer other size groupings, including those over five feet eleven inches.

In addition to the chain of stores that features all special-size categories and issues mail order catalogs, there are other chains of stores that sell clothing for tall women exclusively. Also, some department stores have special "tall clothes departments." For those who prefer to make their clothes, patterns are available in women's sizes proportioned for the tall figure.

Clothing for tall men appeared on the market at approximately the same time as clothing for tall women, and there is a chain of stores for tall and large men which also issues a mail order catalog. The retail stores in this chain are located in the major eastern and midwestern cities, and some manufacturers make some lines of clothing proportioned for tall and large men which are carried in a number of men's clothing stores.

Short Stature

Women of moderately short stature may find that half-sizes satisfy their needs, or they may purchase regular sizes and make the necessary alterations. In men's wear, other than custom-made and made-to-measure garments, those in regular sizes must be altered, particularly the shortening of trousers and sleeves.

People of extremely short stature are classified as either midgets or dwarfs. *Midgets* rarely grow taller than three feet four inches but they are perfectly proportioned and may be called "miniatures" of persons of normal stature. In addition to being short, male midgets usually lack beards and female midgets are generally small breasted. Their reduced stature is thought to be, in part at least, the result of malfunctioning pituitary glands which control growth and, indirectly, secondary sexual characteristics. *Dwarfs* are little people who are disproportioned, with nearly normal torsos, short arms and legs, large heads with prominent foreheads, recessed noses and often bowed legs. The majority of dwarfs are from three feet four inches to four feet, eight inches in height.[14]

Though there is no exact count of the number of midgets and dwarfs in the population, it is estimated by medical authorities that there are about 100,000, which is less than 1/20 of 1 percent of the population of the United States. Therefore, these extremely short people do not constitute a large enough market to make commercial production of clothing for them economically feasible. Satisfying their clothing needs thus becomes one of their major problems, and it is not surprising that clothing is one of the subjects much discussed by midgets and dwarfs when the Little People of America attend their annual meetings. Organized in 1957, the Little People of America, started by Billy Bartz who is a dwarf actor, has about 2500 members and has its official headquarters at Owatonna, Minnesota. Anyone who is four feet ten inches or shorter may join the LPA. The motto of the LPA is "think big."[14, 15]

Purchasing Ready-Made Clothing

Midgets do not have as great difficulty in satisfying their clothing needs as do dwarfs of equal height. Midgets can purchase children's clothing, though styles, decoration, and fabrics used are often inappropriate for adult midgets. Small size shoes available may be only children's styles, though there is less difference, at present, between styles in shoes for children and those for adults as there was some years ago.

In addition to being very short, dwarfs have the added problem of being disproportioned. When ready-made clothing is purchased in sizes to fit horizontal and girth measurements, the most needed alterations are in the shortening of sleeves, skirts, and trousers. In the shortening of sleeves with elbow fitting, the alteration must include raising the elbow to fit the short upper arm.

Some adult dwarfs and midgets do not like to wear altered children's clothing because they want very much to be recognized as adults. Because of their short stature, it is easy for other people to still look upon them as children. While fit is the most important factor in clothing, durability is also important. Furniture is proportioned for people of average height and short people cannot seat themselves on chairs and get up as easily as people of average height. They have to slide on and off chairs and other seating facilities which causes much abrasion and thus wear.

Clothing Advice from LPA

The handbook published by the LPA offers advice on clothing to maximize the appearance of height and to make the short figure more attractive. Short people are advised to keep the silhouette simple with little detail, to use smooth flat fabrics in either solid colors or very small patterns, and to use one color for dresses and suits rather than two-color combinations to give the illusion of greater height. It is suggested that they avoid very high neck garments such as turtle-neck types, skirts that are very full or very straight and narrow, puffed sleeves and shoulder pads, and much trim that detracts from the silhouette. Also, they are advised against the use of oversize accessories such as jewelry, scarves, and handbags.[16]

A recent source of practical help in solving the clothing problems of "little people" was a clothing workshop conducted at the 1977 national meeting of the LPA in Portland, Oregon, by Linda A. Thiel, Assistant Professor of Clothing, Textiles and Related Art in the School of Home Economics at the

Oregon State University.[17]

Female Dwarfs

In further effort to give the illusion of height, slightly raised waistlines in dresses are better than waistlines placed at the natural waistlines. Also, in two-piece dresses or suits, short tops or jackets add to the illusion of height, rather than long tops and jackets which tend to carry the eye downward. Hair styles and hats should be selected with consideration of the effect on the total stature. Bouffant hair styles are not good for dwarfs since they exaggerate the size of the already large head and further emphasize the disproportionate size of the head. Hair styles that keep the hair close to the head are more appropriate. In the selection of hats, it might be tempting to select tall styles in an effort to add height to the figure, but such styles would also add to the apparent size of the head and make the figure appear top heavy. The best hat styles for dwarfs are those that fit closely to the head, with little decoration other than a feather extending upward, and in the same color as the outer garments with which the hat is worn.[16]

Because of the difficulty of finding ready-made clothing which can be readily altered to fit, much of the clothing for female dwarfs must be made by them or for them by dressmakers and tailors. For those who make their own clothing, and for dressmakers and tailors who make clothing for dwarfs, one way to add to the efficiency of the total process is to first make a basic pattern to fit the individual in order to avoid the necessity of always going through the whole process of pattern alteration each time a garment is made. Principles of pattern making are described and illustrated in textbooks on pattern making and can be used in making basic patterns to fit the proportions of dwarfs.

Male Dwarfs

Male dwarfs have much the same clothing problem as female dwarfs as a result of their short and disproportioned stature.

Most male dwarfs have their outer garments, such as suits and coats, custom-made by tailors who specialize in this category of tailoring. Custom-mades are made by the tailor who takes the measurements and makes the garments. These tailors usually provide for fittings during the process of tailoring to insure that the finished garment will fit perfectly. Made-to-measure tailoring is done in factories which receive orders from tailors or retailors who send the necessary measurements and specifications concerning style, fabric, color, and whatever other special considerations that should be noted for the individual customer.[16]

Another source of clothing to meet the needs of male dwarfs is altered ready-made clothing, including boys' "husky" sizes which are said to be more easily adaptable to the proportions of dwarfs than other size categories. To give the greatest illusion of height, it is best to avoid the use of plaids or horizontal stripes, and to select solid colors in medium and deep shades. Very narrow vertical stripes may be slenderizing and may add to the illusion of greater height.

The alterations needed on coats and jackets always include the shortening and narrowing of sleeves. Shortened sleeves must be tapered to fit, and where there is elbow fitting, it must be raised to conform to the length of the upper arm. Coats and jackets must be shortened, and because it is difficult to raise most tailored pockets, garments with patch pockets should be selected so that the raising of the pockets can be achieved more easily.

In trousers and slacks, the alteration for reducing the waistline must be made at the center back seam, and if the rise from the crotch to the top of the trousers or slacks is too long, the alteration should be made at the top of the garment. Garments of this kind that need to be shortened must be tapered on both inseams and outside leg seams beginning at the crotch.

The main clothing problem of dwarfs, in their early childhood, is adaptation to shorter stature and shorter arms, but in adolescence, the problem of finding suitable ready-made clothes becomes very frustrating and adds to psychosocial stress, especially for boys to whom height appearance has more meaning than for girls.[18]

One easy way for all short people to add to the appearance of greater height is to wear shoes with high heels. However, medium height heels are better because the posture of short people may be adversely affected by the wearing of high heels. In addition to short feet, dwarfs have a problem that midgets do not have in finding shoes that fit. Dwarfs' feet are wide for their length, so children's shoes do not fit. In order to get sufficient width, they sometimes have to purchase larger sizes and stuff the toes with paper to fill out the extra length. Otherwise, shoes must be custom-made or obtained from a source which specializes in unusual sizes.

REFERENCES

1. Dnyder, Ruth: What's important is, you're alive. *Du Pont Magazine,* *69*(2):21-23, March-April, 1975.

2. Lasser, Terese: *Reach To Recovery.* New York, American Cancer Society, 1974.

3. Wain, Harry: *The Story Behind the Word — Some Interesting Origins of Medical Terms.* Springfield, Thomas, 1958.

4. Zeissler, Renate H., Rose, Gertrude B., and Nelson, Paul A.: Postmastectomy lymphedema: late results of treatment of 385 patients. *Archives of Physical Medicine and Rehabilitation, 53*(4):159-166, April, 1972.

5. *Instructions for the Patient with Urinary Diversions.* Iowa City, Department of Nursing, University of Iowa Hospitals and Clinics, 1973.

6. *Ostomy Quarterly.* United Ostomy Association, Los Angeles, Fall, 1977.

7. Masland, Richard: New hope for epileptics — but we still have a long way to go. *U. S. News and World Report,* 53-55, September 5, 1977.

8. *Answers to the Most Frequent Questions about Epilepsy.* Washington, D.C., Epilepsy Foundation of America, 1976.

9. Mueller, James L.: Personal communication, November 8, 1977. (Research Designer, Division of Rehabilitation Medicine, George Washington University Medical Center)

10. Hartford, C. E. and Boyd, W. C.: Thermal injury. Leighty, R. D. and Soper, R. T.: *Synopsis of Surgery,* 3rd ed. St. Louis, Mosby, 1975.

11. Malick, Maude H.: Management of the severely burned patient. *British Journal of Occupational Therapy, 38*(4):76-80, April, 1975.

12. *A Step-by-Step Guide to Personal Management for Blind Persons.* New York, American Foundation for the Blind, 1970.

13. *Understanding Braille*. New York, American Foundation for the Blind, 1970.
14. Weinberg, Martin S.: The problems of midgets and dwarfs and organizational remedies: a study of the Little People of America. *Journal of Health and Social Behavior, 9*:65-71, September, 1968.
15. Kleinfield, Sonny: Dwarfs. *Atlantic Monthly, 238*(9):62-66, September, 1975.
16. *Clothes Make the Man/Woman — If You Can Find Them. LPA Handbook*. Little People of America, Owatonna, Minnesota, 1971.
17. Thiel, Linda A.: *Little People — Big Problems*. Paper presented at national meeting of the Association of College Professors of Textiles and Clothing. Dallas, Texas, October 4, 1977.
18. Bailey, Joseph A.: *Disproportionate Short Stature — Diagnosis and Management*. Philadelphia, Saunders, 1973.

Chapter 9

SOLUTION TO CLOTHING PROBLEMS: CHALLENGE AND OPPORTUNITY

THE feeling of self-confidence, the sense of well-being and of social acceptance that comes from the wearing of clothing that is functional, appropriate, and attractive, is important to all people, but to those with physical limitations, it is much more important. Those, who have suffered physical losses need to make the most of the positive values of clothing. In addition to providing greater comfort and facilitating dressing and undressing, the right clothing will make them feel more like their ideal selves, will enhance their self-esteem, and help to bring out abilities they did not know they had, despite the trauma of physical limitations, pain, and uncertainty.

ROLE OF HOME ECONOMISTS

Initiative for services in the field of clothing for those with special needs should come from home economists, because home economics is the only profession that claims clothing design, construction, and adaptation as a part of its area of specialization and expertise. In the commercial production of clothing, there are many highly skilled clothing designers and operators in the various processes of manufacturing whose training and orientation is geared to the mass market and not to the limited market for those who, because of physical limitations, have special clothing needs. Others who may be skilled in the field of clothing construction are women in the communities who have learned largely from secondary school courses, their mothers, local adult education classes, and other community resources, but are concerned primarily with the making of clothing for people in normal physical condition. In

151

some hospitals and rehabilitation centers, home economists are serving as members of rehabilitation teams and are providing an indispensable service as they supplement the work of health-related professional personnel. In the total rehabilitation process, many kinds of skills are needed rather than only those of one physician.

Just as important as serving on rehabilitation teams is concern for the needs of individuals in the communities, especially those who are far removed from health facilities and the services of therapists and other health-oriented specialists. There are many people in need in the communities who do not benefit from services of any kind because of the lack of knowledge of resources, transportation problems, or their own low estimation of their personal worth and the possibility of improvement in their quality of life. In addition to giving help directly to individuals in communities, home economists may find opportunities to be of service at the community, district, and the state levels in agencies concerned with the aged, and also in the many organizations concerned with the physically handicapped and the mentally retarded and with the many organized groups of parents of physically handicapped and mentally retarded children. Services to these groups may include general information, consultative service and instruction in the selection of clothing, adaptation of garments in current wardrobes and in ready-made garments, and in alteration of patterns for making clothing at home.

To be of greatest service in this field, home economists need basic knowledge of textiles, clothing design, selection and construction of clothing, and knowledge of the physical limitations of the chronically ill, the aged, the physically handicapped, the mentally retarded, and those with other physical conditions that bring about special clothing needs. Home economists who provide help, need to recognize the psychological problems which may be involved in order to understand the immediate reaction of the people concerned. Attitudes toward the self, toward other people and even toward life could affect interest in clothing and the acceptance or rejection of help offered in dealing with clothing problems.

In addition to basic knowledge in the field of clothing, very much practical information may be gained from visits to health-related facilities for observation and consultation concerning clothing needs. This would also help in developing greater understanding of physical limitations, more interest in people in need, and greater ease in approaching those who are different. In order to disseminate information most broadly on clothing for those with special needs, courses in clothing offered by home economists at both the secondary school level and in institutions of higher learning should include some basic information in the field of special clothing needs, which could be put into practice by the students in their own families and in their communities.

Difficulties in solving clothing problems sometimes may lead to frustration as patients or other individuals in need, who may be very discouraged, may not be receptive to new ideas about clothing, but when frustration blocks further effort much may be lost. In such situations, one needs to deal with frustration rather than give in to it, and use frustration as challenges, opportunities, and gateways to progress. The message to take courage and carry on is found in the words of Elbert Hubbard who said, "Go as far as you can see, and when you get there, you will see further." In looking back, after climbing half way up a hill, the grade does not ever look as steep as it did from the bottom. In responding to challenges, we discover new dimensions of our own abilities, and our achievements inspire the efforts and contributions of others. New solutions evolve as people become more perceptive and concentrate their energies and inventiveness on unique clothing problems.

FAMILY NEEDS

In almost every family, there will be someone, at some time, who will need clothing adapted to unusual physical conditions, and almost everyone will have a friend or neighbor with similar needs. In families where there is a physically handicapped child who cannot cope with regular clothing, the mother may dress and undress the child to save time, and thus, the child may never learn to get along without help. Adapted, manageable clothing could solve such a problem. Attitudes of over-protection and constant help tend to nurture dependency of the person involved whether an adult or child, which could increase the burden on the family.

Some families may not believe that clothing is of much importance to one who is chronically ill, merely old, physically handicapped or mentally retarded, that clothing can be adapted for those with various limitations or that anyone in the community could have any interest in the needs of members of their families. Home economists, with adequate knowledge and ability in this field, could open up new vistas of possibilities to such families.

HUMAN VALUES

Those who help others in need of special clothing must have faith in themselves and in those they help. Confidence in one's knowledge and ability will be communicated to those they help, who, in turn, will develop motivation and eventually achieve the seemingly impossible in terms of the activities of daily living. Some of the people who need help with clothing may be suffering from pain and depression and may be feeling very much alone. There may be breakdowns in their relationships to family, friends, and society, and they may have reached a very low ebb of life. Improvements in clothing and solving of some of the difficult problems should help those in need to see themselves in a new light that encourages their own ingenuity and opens up to them new avenues of thought and possibilities.[1]

Better appearance through improvement of clothing will help to develop inner resources that will be sustaining in periods of depression and will help people to believe that they have worth in the sight of others and in their own view of themselves. What most of these people need is a feeling of greater possibilities for themselves in which their adequacies are emphasized and their intelligence is brought into play. Having clothing that meets their needs and that looks like the clothing worn by other people, they may be more readily integrated into the family activity and other social activity.

Often, great tragedy and severe illness brings about deeper views of life, greater insights, depths of understanding, and appreciation. Nonhandicapped persons who offer help can sometimes learn from the handicapped the lessons that come from the experience of tragedy and values based not as much on material things as those of the mind and the spirit, all of which provide a philosophical approach in the solution to practical problems. Doctor Harold H. Wilkie discovered solutions to clothing problems not known to anyone else. In *Using Everything You've Got,* Dr. Wilkie, who is armless, a Harvard graduate and an ordained minister, married and the father of five children, tells how he manages his clothing and other activities of daily living, including much travel.

It is by deeds that we express the ideals and commitments we claim, and in helping others to meet their special clothing needs, we may help to replace despair with hope. We enhance our own sense of personal worth as we serve the needs of others either on a paid or volunteer basis. A philosophy of possibilities finds "what can be done" rather than "what can't be done." An individual may ask, "What can I do? I'm only one person." The answer is that it takes only one person with an idea to initiate a new concept in serving the needs of people. *A World To Care For* is an account of the efforts of Doctor Rusk in applying a philosophy of possibilities to rehabilitation which brought into being a new branch of medicine — physical medicine and rehabilitation. Home economists may consider doing something similar in the field of special clothing needs.

REFERENCE

1. Bonner, Charles D.: *Medical Care and Rehabilitation of the Aged and Chronically Ill.* Boston, Little, 1974.

APPENDICES

Appendix A

SELECTED ADDITIONAL READINGS

BOOKS

An Introduction to Working with the Aging Person Who is Visually Handicapped. New York, American Foundation for the Blind, 1972.

Bader, Iva M.: Clothing for the elderly. In *Working with Older People* (A Guide to Practice, Vol. III, THE Aging Person: Needs and Services). Washington, D.C. Public Health Service, Department of Health, Education and Welfare, 1970.

Bare, Clari, Boettke, Eleanor, and Waggoner, Neva: *Self-Help Clothing for Handicapped Children.* Chicago, National Society for Crippled Children and Adults, 1962.

Brown, Mary Eleanor: Self-help clothing. In Licht, Sidney Herman (Ed.): *Orthotics.* Baltimore, Williams & Wilkens, 1966, chap. 25.

Cookman, Helen and Zimmerman, Muriel E.: *Functional Fashions for the Physically Handicapped.* New York, Institute of Rehabilitation Medicine, New York University Medical Center, 1961.

Davies, Marcella Zaleski: *Living with Multiple Sclerosis: A Social and Psychological Analysis.* Springfield, Thomas, 1973.

Encyclopedia of Associations, 11th ed. Detroit, Gale Research Company, 1977.

Fishbein, Morris: *Birth Defects.* New York, Lippincott, 1963.

Gibson, David and Brown, Roy J.: *Managing the Severely Retarded: A Sampler.* Springfield, Thomas, 1976.

Gilbert, Arlene E.: *You Can Do It from a Wheelchair.* New Rochelle, Arlington House, 1973.

Goffman, Irving: *Stigma: Notes on the Management of Spoiled Identity.* Englewood Cliffs, P-H, 1963.

Greenblott, Milton: *From Custodial to Therapeutic Care in Mental Hospitals.* New York, Russell Sage, 1965.

Henderson, Shirley and McDonald, Mary: *Step-by-Step Dressing — A Handbook for Teaching the Retarded to Dress.* Champaign, Suburban Publications, 1973.

Koch, Richard and De La Cruz, Felix F. (Eds.): *Down's Syndrome: Research, Prevention and Management.* New York, Brunner-Mazel, 1975.

Krusen, Frank H., Kottke, Frederick J., and Ellwood, Paul M.: *Handbook of Physical Medicine and Rehabilitation.* Philadelphia, Saunders, 1955.

Lowenfeld, Berthold: *Our Blind Children: Growing and Learning with*

Them. Springfield, Thomas, 1971.

May, Elizabeth Eckhardt, Waggoner, Neva R., and Hotte, Eleanor Boettke: *Independent Living for the Handicapped and the Elderly.* Boston, Houghton Mifflin, 1974.

Rusk, Howard A.: *Rehabilitation Medicine.* St. Louis, Mosby, 1958.

Self-Care for the Hemiplegic. Minneapolis, Sister Kenny Institute, 1970.

Willington, F. L. (Ed.): *Incontinence in the Elderly.* New York, Acad Pr, 1976.

Winkler, Win Ann: *Post Mastectomy: A Personal Guide to Physical and Emotional Recovery.* New York, Hawthorn, 1976.

ARTICLES

Ahrbeck, Ellen Henselmann and Friend, Shirley: Clothing — an asset or liability? Designing for special needs. *Rehabilitation Literature, 37*(10):295-296, 320, October 1976.

Bader, Iva M. and Hoffman, Adeline M.: Research in aging. *Journal of Home Economics, 58*(1):9-14, January 1966.

Beppler, Marcia C.: The disabled homemaker: organizational activities, family participation, and rehabilitation success. *Rehabilitation Literature, 35*(7):200-206, July 1974.

Boettke, Eleanor M. and Zook, Margaret: Dress design with self-help features for the pre-school child. *Journal of Home Economics, 48*(8):643-646, October 1956.

Broome, Charlotte: Fashions for the physically handicapped woman. *The Canadian Nurse, 71*(11):18-22, November 1975.

Brown, Mary Eleanor: Fashions for the C.P.'s. *Cerebral Palsy Review, 12*(8):4-5, 8, September 1951.

Burk, Richard D.: Three value systems. *Journal of Rehabilitation, 37*(1):27-29, January-February 1971.

Cailliet, Rene: Care of common foot problems. *American Family Physician, 2*(5):101-108, November 1970.

Cautels, Joseph R. and Flannery, Raymond R.: Seizures: Controlling the uncontrollable. *Journal of Rehabilitation, 39*(3):34-35, 39, May-June 1973.

Dillingham, Elizabeth: Feeding and dressing techniques for the cerebral palsied child. *Crippled Child, 26*(12):20-22, 29, December 1948.

Friend, Shirley E.: Meeting the clothing needs of handicapped children. *Journal of Home Economics, 65*(5):25-27, May 1973.

Goldberg, Richard T.: Rehabilitation of the burn patient. *Rehabilitation Literature, 35*(3):73-78, March 1974.

Hall, Dorothy S. and Vignos, Paul J.: Clothing adaptations for the child with progressive muscular dystrophy. *American Journal of Occupational Therapy, XVIII*(3):108-112, May-June 1964.

Hartwig, Eugene C., Wenzel, Frederick J., and Hintz, Charles S.: Maxillofacial protective headgear. *Orthotics and Prosthetics, 31*(1):25-28, March 1977.

Helfand, Author E.: Podiatry — a basic long-term need for the chronically ill and the aged. *Nursing Home, 42*(6):9-10, June 1963.

Hoffman, Adeline M. and Bader, Iva M.: Clothing — common denominator between the young and the old. *Gerontologist, 14*(5):437-439, October 1974.

Mathias, Charles McC.: Rehabilitation — the challenge, past and present. *Journal of Rehabilitation, 42*(1):18-20, January-February 1976.

Maxwell, Richard: Quadriplegia: What does it mean? *Journal of Rehabilitation, 37*(3):10-13, May-June 1971.

Newton, Audrey: Clothing — a rehabilitation tool for the handicapped. *Journal of Home Economics, 65*(4):29-30, April 1973.

Newton, Audrey: Clothing: a positive part of the rehabilitation process. *Journal of Rehabilitation, 42*(5):18-22, September-October 1976.

O'Conner, Joseph R. and Leitner, Lewis A.: Traumatic quadriplegia — a comprehensive view. *Journal of Rehabilitation, 37*(3):14-20, May-June 1971.

Reich, Naomi: Clothing for the handicapped and disabled. *Rehabilitation Literature, 37*(10):290-294, October 1976.

Rikert, Gladys, Sloane, Nancy, Sosnowski, Gloria, and Weincrot, Bernice: Dressing techniques for the cerebral palsied child. *American Journal of Occupational Therapy, 8*(1):8-10, 37, January-February 1954.

Runge, Margaret: Self-dressing techniques for patients with spinal cord injury. *American Journal of Occupational Therapy, 21*(6):367-375, November-December 1967.

Rusk, Howard A. and Taylor, Eugene J.: Functional fashions for the physically handicapped. *Journal of the American Medical Association, 169*(14):138-140, April 1959.

Schuster, Jan D. and Kelly, Donice H.: Preferred style features in dresses for physically handicapped elderly women. *Gerontologist, 14*(2):106-109, April 1974.

Schwab, Lois O.: The home economist in rehabilitation. *Rehabilitation Literature, 29*(5):130-136, 138, May 1968.

Schwab, Lois O. and Sindelar, Margaret B.: Clothing for physically handicapped homemakers. *Rehabilitation Record, 14*(2):30-34, March-April 1973.

Schwab, Lois O. and Knoll, Cecelia Sue: The outlook for home economists in rehabilitation. *Journal of Home Economics, 66*(1):39-42, January 1974.

Scott, Clarice L.: Clothing needs for physically handicapped homemakers. *Journal of Home Economics, 51*(8):709-713, October 1959.

Siller, Jerome: Psychological situation of the disabled with spinal cord injuries. *Rehabilitation Literature, 30*(10):290-296, October 1969.

Travelbee, Joyce: Speaking out — to find meaning in illness. *Nursing, 2*(12):6-8, December 1972.

Wagner, Elizabeth M., Kunstadter, Ralph H., and Shover, Jayne: Self-help clothing for handicapped children. *Clinical Pediatrics, 2*(3):122-126, March 1963.

Warden, Jessie and Dedman, Krista: Clothing design, uses, styles, and utility.

Journal of Rehabilitation, 41(4):17-19, July-August 1975.

Wax, John: The inner life — a new dimension of rehabilitation. *Journal of Rehabilitation, 38*(6):16-18, November-December 1972.

Yep, Jacquelyn Orlando: Tools for aiding physically disabled individuals increase independence in dressing. *Journal of Rehabilitation, 43*(5):39-41, December 1977.

THESES AND DISSERTATIONS

Allen, Cynthia Jean: *Clothing Design for the Physically Handicapped Elderly Woman.* Master's Thesis, Bozeman, Montana State University, 1975.

Bader, Iva M.: *An Exploratory Study of Clothing Problems and Attitudes of a Group of Older Women in Iowa City, Iowa.* Master's Thesis, Iowa City, University of Iowa, 1963.

Coyle, Anne B.: *A Study of the Clothing Needs and Clothing Desires of Older Women in a Selected Area of Rhode Island.* Master's Thesis, Kingston, University of Rhode Island, 1964.

Dallas, Mary Jo: *Daytime Dresses for Teenage Girls and Young Adults with Cerebral Palsy.* Master's Thesis, Fort Collins, Colorado State University, 1965.

Feather, Betty L.: *The Relationship Between the Self-Concept and Clothing Attitudes of Physically Handicapped and Able Bodied University Men and Women.* Doctoral Dissertation, Columbia, University of Missouri, 1976.

Fresdura, Lynda Glee: *Clothing for Girls with Specified Physical Handicaps.* Master's Thesis, Corvallis, Oregon State University, 1963.

Houston, Peggy Stiles: *Changes in Clothing Behavior of Older Rural Women.* Master's Thesis, Iowa City, University of Iowa, 1965.

Jacobson, Martha Lucille: *Guidelines for a Patient-Oriented Clothing Center in a State Mental Institution.* Master's Thesis, Carbondale, Southern Illinois University, 1967.

Jonson, Joyce E.: *Play Garments for Disabled Children.* Master's Thesis, Fort Collins, Colorado State University, 1972.

Madsen, Jean Kersten: *Adaptation of Daytime Dresses for Women with Rheumatoid Arthritis.* Master's Thesis, Lafayette, Ind, Purdue University, 1967.

Massey, Frances Wilson: *Clothing Needs of Women Over 65 Years of Age.* Master's Thesis, University of North Carolina at Greensboro, 1964.

McQuire, Leota Mahauta: *The Design and Evaluation of Selected Garments for the Cerebral Palsied Female Child.* Master's Thesis, Norman, University of Oklahoma, 1970.

Miller, Mary McLeran: *Clothing Behavior of Women Residing in Retirement Homes.* Master's Thesis, Iowa City, University of Iowa, 1968.

Motley, Verna G.: *An Exploratory Study of Dress and Grooming Habits of Moderately Mentally Retarded Youth with Implications for Curriculum Planning.* Master's Thesis, College Park, University of

Maryland, 1968.

Rice, Virginia Ketterfield: *Attractive Garment Designs for Physically Handicapped Women Who Wear Long Leg Braces and Who Use Crutches.* Master's Thesis, Tallahassee, Florida State University, 1971.

Richardson, Nancy: *Dramatic and Play Clothes for Pre-School Physically Handicapped Boys Wearing Long Leg Braces.* Master's Thesis, College Park, University of Maryland, 1971.

Shaw, Linda: *Social Motivation and Clothing Selection Problems of the Classic Achondroplastic Dwarf.* Master's Thesis, Corvallis, Oregon State University, 1976.

Sindelar, Margaret: *Clothing Satisfactions and Preferences of Physically Disabled Homemakers.* Master's Thesis, University of Nebraska at Lincoln, 1970.

Smiley, Cleretta Henderson: *Clothing Perceptions of Early Adolescent Girls with Physical Abnormalities and Orthopedic Physical Disabilities.* Master's Thesis, College Park, University of Maryland, 1971.

Taylor, Lois Pickens: *Dresses and a Coat for Physically Handicapped Girls Ages Five Through Twelve, Who Use Braces, Crutches, and Wheelchairs.* Master's Thesis, Morgantown, West Virginia University, 1963.

Yep, Jacquelyn Orlando: *Preparation of Extension Home Economists as Clothing Consultants to Physically Disabled Individuals.* Doctoral Dissertation, Ames, Iowa State University, 1976.

Zaccagnini, Judith: *Adaptive Fasteners for Ready-to-Wear Knit Pullover Shirts for Children with Cerebral Palsy.* Master's Thesis, Manhattan, Kansas State University, 1970.

BIBLIOGRAPHIES

Beasley, Mary Catherine, Burns, Dorothy, and Weiss, Janis M.: *Resource Materials on Clothing and Rehabilitation.* University, University of Alabama, On YOUR OWN program, Continuing Education in Home Economics, Division of Continuing Education, 1977.

Berdahl, Ella Mae: *A Selected Bibliography on Handicapped.* Home Economics Extension Service, USDA, Washington, D.C., 1977.

Hoffman, Adeline M. and Bader, Iva M.: *Social Science Aspects of Clothing for Older Women: An Annotated Bibliography,* 2nd ed. Iowa City, University of Iowa, Division of Continuing Education and Department of Home Economics, 1977.

Newton, Audrey, Nelson, Barbara Ann, and Odu, Dorcas: *Clothing for the Elderly: An Annotated Bibliography.* University of Nebraska at Lincoln, Agricultural Experiment Station, 1975.

Schwab, Lois O.: *Homemaker Rehabilitation: A Selected Bibliography.* President's Committee on Employment of the Handicapped, Washington, D.C., 1977.

Yost, Anna Catherine, Schroeder, Stella L., and Rainey, Carolyn: *Home*

Economics Rehabilitation: A Selected Annotated Bibliography. Columbia, University of Missouri, College of Home Economics, 1977.

Zimmerman, Muriel E.: *Clothing for the Disabled.* New York, New York University Medical Center, Department of Occupational Therapy, Institute of Rehabilitation Medicine, 1976.

BRITISH PUBLICATIONS

Forbes, Gillian: *Clothing for the Handicapped Child.* The Disabled Living Foundation. 346 Kennsington High Street, London W14, England, 1971.

Gamwell, Ann W. and Joyce, Florence: *Problems of Clothing for the Sick and Disabled — In Hospital and Community, including Elderly, Infirm, and Mentally Retarded.* Central Council for the Disabled, 39 Victoria Street, London, S.W.1. England, 1966.

Macartney, P.: *Clothes Sense for Handicapped Adults of All Ages.* The Disabled Living Foundation, 1973.

Ruston, Rosemary: *Dressing for the Disabled.* The Disabled Living Foundation, 1977.

Clothing Project Staff: *How to Adapt Existing Clothing for the Disabled.* The Disabled Living Foundation, 1971.

Clothing Panel: *Clothing Fasteners for the Handicapped and Disabled.* The Disabled Living Foundation, 1968.

Hasbec, I. and Wright, V.: Footwear for arthritic patients. *Annals of Physical Medicine,* February 1970.

Malick, Maude H.: Management of the severely burned patient. *British Journal of Occupational Therapy, 38*:4, April 1975.

Rogers, E. E. and Stevens, B. M.: Dressmaking for the disabled. *Occupational Therapy,* January, February, March, April, and May, 1966.

OTHER PUBLICATIONS

Beasley, M. C., Burns, D. B., and Weiss, J. M.: *Adapt Your Own.* University, University of Alabama, Continuing Education Division, 1977.

Common Questions About Fire and Burns. Shriners Burn Institute, Boston, Massachusetts, 1974.

Hallenbeck, Phyllis N., Skipper, James K., and Fink, Stephen L.: *How the Severely Disabled Client Perceives the Problems of Daily Living.* Final Report of VRA Project No. RD-1584, Vocational Guidance and Rehabilitation Services, Cleveland, Ohio, 1966.

Caddel, Kay: *Measurements, Guidelines and Solutions* (in the fitting of clothing), a manual for solving clothing problems for persons with physical disabilities. Lubbock, Vintage Press, 1977.

McDonald, Kathryn, Dardis, Rachel, and Smith, B. F.: *Investigation of Textile Fires in a Selected Area of New York State.* Proceedings of the

Third Annual Meeting, Information Council on Fabric Flammability, December 4, 1969.

Miranda, Rose, and von Czeh, Irene (Eds.): *Home Economics: Meeting the Needs of the Elderly.* Proceedings of the Fifth Annual Conference for Home Economists, Hunter College Department of Home Economics of the City University of New York, 1975.

Schwab, Lois O.: Proceedings — *Training Institute for Rehabilitation Teachers of the Blind: Teaching the Newly Blinded Homemaker.* University of Nebraska at Lincoln, College of Home Economics and Rehabilitation Services Administration, 1970.

Wilke, Harold H.: *Using Everything You've Got.* Chicago, The National Easter Seal Society for Crippled Children and Adults, 1977.

Rehabilitation of the Physically Handicapped in Homemaking Activities. Proceedings of a Workshop, Vocational Rehabilitation Administration, Department of Health, Education and Welfare, 1963.

Convenience Clothing and Closures. New York, Talon/Velcro Consumer Education, 1975.

Appendix B

SOURCES OF CLOTHING, FOOTWEAR, AND OTHER SPECIAL NEEDS

Amputee Shoe and Glove Exchange, 1635 Warwickshire Drive, Houston, Texas 77077

Information exchange to facilitate swaps of unneeded shoes and gloves by amputees. Attempts to match amputees who need the opposite shoe and glove, who are about the same age, and who have reasonably similar tastes. All mailing of shoes and gloves are between amputees matched. The exchange serves men, women, and children.

Damart, Inc., 2450 West Sibley Blvd., Posen, Illinois 69469

Thermolactyl underwear for men and women to provide special comfort in cold weather.

Danmar Products, Inc., 2390 Winewood, Ann Arbor, Michigan 48103

Manufacturers of Wolverine Brand protective helmets designed exclusively for institutional use. Catalog available with detailed description, price list, and information for ordering.

Fashion-Able, Rocky Hill, New Jersey 08553

Clothing for physically handicapped women and self-help items for independent living.

Fingerprint Patterns, 155 Belaire Avenue, Louisville, Kentucky 40206

Catalog of patterns for the blind, made of heavy brown paper with raised lines to indicate grain, darts and other markings, and with instructions in Braille.

Geri Fashions, 301 E. Illinois Street, Newberg, Oregon 97132

Garments designed for comfort and ease of dressing for women confined to wheelchairs.

Ger-Specials, 9201 Shawnee Shores, Coldwater, Michigan 49036

Garments for older men and women by Evelyn Reedy Industries.

Handee for You, 7674 Park Avenue, Lowville, New York 13367

Semi-custom-made clothing for women with physical handicaps.

Helen's Shoe Service, Route 4, Red Wing, Minnesota 55066

A shoe service for men and women who wear two different shoe sizes or need only one shoe. A file of information provides matching possibilities, and correspondence is carried on between those who have shoes available and those who need them to facilitate exchange.

Jobst Institute, Inc., P. O. Box 653, Toledo, Ohio 43694

Jobst burn supports and elastic sleeves, and gauntlets for mastectomy patients with edema.

Karoll's, Inc., Institution Division, 32 N. State Street, Chicago, Illinois 60602

Specialists in clothing for men, women, and children in mental hospitals, and for children in schools for the mentally retarded. In addition to illustrations, the catalog gives descriptions and a measurement chart to assure accuracy in fitting of garments. Incontinence items for children and adults are included in the catalog.

Designs by Kay Caddel, Textiles Research Center, P. O. Box 4150, Lubbock, Texas 79409

Patterns for clothing for the physically handicapped and mentally retarded, produced through the Textiles Research Center, Texas Tech University, Lubbock, Texas, in cooperation with the Natural Fibers and Protein Commission of Texas.

The King Size Co., 4115 King-Size Building, Brockton, Massachusetts 02402

A chain of eighteen stores in the metropolitan areas in eastern and midwestern states, that specialize in all clothing items for large and tall men, and shoes up to size 16. The King Size Co. also issues a mail order catalog.

Lane Bryant, Inc., 1501 Broadway, New York, New York 10036 Mail order catalog address is Lane Bryant, Inc., 2300 Southeastern Avenue, Box 7203, Indianapolis, Indiana 46272

A national chain of women's speciality stores, more than 215 in number, which deal exclusively in contemporary fashions for the hard to fit woman and girl. Size ranges include: Women's 38-56; Half sizes 14 1/2-32 1/2; Minums for women five feet two inches and under, 12M-26M; Junior Plenty 15-27; Chubby Girls 8 1/2-16 1/2; Chubby Teens 11 1/2-17 1/2; and Tall Girls 10-22 for those five feet seven inches and taller, and shoes up to size 13. Some stores carry large size maternity wear 18-46.

(Lane Bryant, Inc. was founded in 1900 by Lane Bryant, a young widowed seamstress who created the first maternity wear.)

"Men's Fashions for the Wheelchair Set," Leinenweber, Inc., Custom Tailors, Brunswick Building, 69 W. Washington Street, Chicago, Illinois 60602

Made-to-measure outer wear for men, proportioned for those confined to wheelchairs.

National Odd Shoe Exchange, Ruth Rubin Feldman, 3100 Neilson Way-220, Santa Monica, California 90401

The National Odd Shoe Exchange, established in 1945, renders a unique service to persons all over the country whose feet are not mates and to persons with only one foot. It serves as a clearinghouse to bring together, by mail, those persons with mutual shoe problems and to aid them in securing serviceable shoes from those in similar situations who have shoes to exchange. The exchange does not deal with shoes, but with the names of persons of similar ages and tastes in shoe styles, who have shoes available or are seeking mismates with whom to exchange extra shoes.

New Look Patient Apparel, Inc., 505 Pearl Street, Buffalo, New York 14202

Specialists in patient apparel that makes for easy dressing of wheelchair patients, rehabilitated and ambulatory patients, and the elderly, both men and women.

P T L Designs, Inc., P. O. Box 364, Stillwater, Oklahoma 74074

Ninety-two items of wearing apparel in sizes for men, women, and children, all custom made. (Mrs. Mary Murphy, President. P T L means "put together with love.")

REACH TO RECOVERY program of the American Cancer Society.

Publishes annually lists of manufacturers of breast prostheses, mastectomy bras, pads, covers, and swim suits, with descriptions, manufacturers' names and addresses, where available, approximate prices, and other information.

Roaman's, 425 Park Avenue, New York, New York 10016

Mail order address is Roaman's, Saddle Brook, New Jersey 07662

A chain of twenty-five women's clothing stores in the metropolitan areas in the eastern states, specializing in fashionable clothing in large sizes, up to size 60. A mail order catalog is issued four times a year, featuring large and half-size garments.

Sarah Soft Wear, Route 1, Red Wing, Minnesota 55066

Appliance covers for ostimates.

Vocational Guidance and Rehabilitation Services, 2239 E. 55th Street, Cleveland, Ohio 44103

Clothing for physically handicapped men, women, and children, including helmets for protection against falling. Catalog "People Helping People Clothing and Aids."

Wheelchair Fashions, Inc., P. O. Box 99, South Windham, Maine 04082

"For the preservation of human dignity" is the maker's motto. Clothing designed for older patients in nursing homes, paraplegics, multiple sclerosis patients, and others who are handicapped and confined to wheelchairs, both men and women.

In addition to the sources listed, others may be found in the classified section (yellow pages) of telephone books in metropolitan areas, particularly regional chains of stores and individual stores that specialize in unusual size ranges in clothing and footwear.

NATIONAL PROFESSIONAL HEALTH RELATED ASSOCIATIONS AND OTHERS WITH SOME CONCERN FOR CLOTHING NEEDS, WITH DATES OF ORGANIZATION*

American Association for Rehabilitation Therapy, P. O. Box 93, North Little Rock, Arkansas 72116

Professional society of medical rehabilitation therapists, specialists, and other interested in vocational rehabilitation of the mentally and physically disabled. To promote the use and advance the practice of curative technical and educational modalities within approved medical concepts of rehabilitation medicine; to establish and advance standards for education and training of rehabilitation therapists and specialists, and to foster study and research. (1950)

American Association on Mental Deficiency (Mental Retardation), 5201 Connecticut Avenue, N. W., Washington, D.C. 20015

Physicians, educators, administrators, social workers, psychologists, psychiatrists, students, and others interested in the general welfare of mentally retarded persons and the study of causes, treatment, and prevention of mental retardation. (1876)

American Burn Association, c/o Dr. Charles E. Hartford, Croter-Chester Medical Center, 15th Street and Upland Avenue, Chester, Pennsylvania 19013

Members are physicians, nurses, physical therapists, occupational therapists, dietitians, biomedical engineers, social service workers, etc., all of whom are interested in the care of patients with burn injuries. Objective is the improvement in the care and treatment of the burn patient, which includes a program of prevention of burn injuries. (1967)

American Cancer Society, 777 Third Avenue, New York, New York 10017

---

*From *Encyclopedia of Associations*, 11th ed. Detroit, Gale Research Co., 1977.

Supports education and research in cancer prevention, diagnosis, detection, and treatment and provides special services to cancer patients. (1913)

American Foundation for the Blind, 15 W. 16th Street, New York, New York 10011

National research, informative, and consultative agency which acts as a clearinghouse for local and regional agencies serving the blind. Sponsors institutes and workshops for professionals working with the blind and visually handicapped persons; records and manufactures talking books for the blind; develops and manufactures special aids for blind persons; conducts public education programs through the mass media; and participates in legislative action and interpretation relative to problems of blindness. (1921)

American Geriatric Society, 10 Columbus Circle, New York, New York 10019

Professional society of physicians, physiotherapists, occupational therapists, social and welfare workers, superintendents of hospitals and homes for the aged, and others interested in the problems of the aged. To encourage and promote the study of geriatrics; to stress the importance of medical research in the field of aging.

American Home Economics Association, 2010 Massachusetts Avenue, N.W., Washington, D.C. 20036

Professional organization of home economists. Works to improve the quality and standards of individual and family life through education, research, cooperative programs, and public information. Its foundation administers funds for AHEA fellowships, traineeships, and international scholarships and supports projects such as workshops, leadership conferences, research, and production of educational materials. Sponsors Center for the Family and Council for Professional Development. (1909)

American Occupational Therapy Association, 600 Executive Boulevard, Suite 200, Rockville, Maryland 20852

Professional society of occupational therapists administering medically supervised activity to persons injured physically or mentally by accident or disease. (1917)

American Physical Therapy Association, 1156 15th Street, N.W., Washington, D.C. 20005

To foster the development and improvement of physical therapy services and physical therapy education, evaluate the organization and administration of curriculum and direct the maintenance of standards and promote scientific research. (1927)

American Podiatry Association, 20 Chevy Chase Circle, N.W., Washington, D.C. 20015

Professional society for podiatrists. Medical and allied health relations, podiatric therapeutists, podiatry education, professional information, footwear. (1912)

The Arthritis Foundation, 3400 Peachtree Rd., N.E., Atlanta, Georgia 30326

To discover the cause and improve the methods for the treatment and prevention of arthritis and other rheumatic diseases; to increase the number of scientists investigating rheumatic diseases; to provide training in rheumatic diseases for more doctors; to extend knowledge of arthritis and other rheumatic diseases to the public, emphasizing socioeconomic as well as medical aspects of the diseases. (1948)

Epilepsy Foundation of America, 1828 L Street, Suite 406, Washington, D.C. 20036

A national voluntary health agency which serves as the focal point for the fight against epilepsy in the United States. Acts as spokesman, advocate, and ombudsman for 4 million Americans with epilepsy. Provides state and federal government liason, defines the myriad problems of these people, and devises specific programs to solve them. Sponsors research in the basic causes of epilepsy, prevention, and improved methods of treatment, and assists in counseling for epilepsy patients through local organizations and a national referral service. (1967)

The Gerontological Society, 1 DuPont Circle, Washington, D.C. 20036

Physicians, physiologists, psychologists, anatomists, biochemists, sociologists, botanists, psychiatrists, pharmacologists, geneticists, zoologists, endocrinologists, administrators, and other professionals interested in improving the well-being of older people by promoting scientific study of the aging process, publishing information about aging and bringing together all groups interested in older people. (1945)

International Society for Prosthetics and Orthotics, 1440 N Street, N.W., Washington, D.C. 20005

Physicians, prosthetists, orthotists, therapists, and rehabilitation engineers. Purposes are to provide high quality orthotic and prosthetic care of all people with neuromuscular and skeletal disabilities and to serve as an international impartial and nonpolitical coordinating advisory body on prosthetics and orthotics. (1973)

Little People of America (LPA), Box 126, Owatonna, Minnesota 55066
Persons of proportionate or disproportionate dwarf types and
others four feet ten inches or under, including children in their
classification of "Little people." Provides fellowship, interchange
of ideas, moral support, and solution to unique problems of little
people; promotes good faith and fair dealing between members and
average size people. Aids in exchange of information on housing,
jobs, clothes, shoes, life insurance, education etc., and sponsors
sports and social activities. Conducts discussions with parents of
average height who have dwarf children; works to bring together
little couples interested in adoption and adoption agencies which
have children of this type available. Cooperates with Moore Clinic,
Johns Hopkins Hospital, Baltimore, Maryland, and many other
medical institutions. Motto of LPA is "think big." (1957)

Muscular Dystrophy Association of America, 1790 Broadway, New
York, New York 10019
Voluntary health agency, fostering research into the cause and cure
of muscular dystrophy and related neuromuscular diseases. Supports international program of research. (1950)

National Association of the Physically Handicapped, 6473 Grand-
ville, Detroit, Michigan 48228
To advance the social, economic, and physical welfare of the physically handicapped; promote rehabilitation and employment opportunities; and make awards to individuals for outstanding service in
the cause of the physically handicapped and to business firms for
outstanding performance in hiring physically handicapped
workers. (1958)

National Council on Obesity, P. O. Box 35306, Los Angeles, California 90035
Purpose is to combat, control, and prevent obesity through education, rehabilitation, and research. Confers with the obese and their
families, offers advice and guidance, and directs those suffering
from the condition to treatment centers, recovery organizations, and
social agencies both public and private to help in coping with the
problems of obesity. Assists business and industry in setting up
labor-management seminars on the subject; helps local companies
formulate policy on industrial obesity and supplies them with educational materials and speakers. Offers services to physicians,
nurses, the clergy, social workers, and vocational counselors whose
work often involves the obese and conducts seminars for them.
Provides professional training in the field of obesity. (1975)

National Easter Seal Society for Crippled Children and Adults, 2023 West Ogden Avenue, Chicago, Illinois 60612

To establish and conduct programs that serve the physically handicapped; work with voluntary and governmental agencies to support services for the handicapped; publish and disseminate information on the needs of the crippled and existing services for them, and on medical and professional activities related to rehabilitation. Maintains library on all aspects of rehabilitation. Operates Easter Seal Research Foundation. (1919)

National Multiple Sclerosis Society, 257 Park Avenue S., New York, New York 10010

To stimulate, support, and coordinate research and treatment and care of multiple sclerosis related disorders of the central nervous system. (1946)

National Rehabilitation Association, 1522 K Street, N.W., Washington, D.C. 20005

Physicians, counselors, therapeutists, disability examiners, vocational evaluators, and others interested in rehabilitation of the physically and mentally handicapped and the socially disadvantaged. (1925)

National Safety Council, 425 N. Michigan Avenue, Chicago, Illinois 60611

Purpose is to reduce the number and severity of all kinds of accidents by gathering and distributing information about the causes of accidents and ways to prevent them. Statistics are supplied by industries, transportation and insurance companies, schools and local safety groups, trade and labor organizations, civic groups, state and federal government departments, international and foreign organizations, and its own staff or statistical, educational, and engineering technicians. (1913)

Sister Kenny Institute, Chicago Avenue at 27th Avenue, Minneapolis, Minnesota 55407

To investigate, evaluate, promote, and support projects in rehabilitation. Compiles statistics on research activities and patient care activities. Specializes in the treatment of acute and chronic disabled patients. Rehabilitation services are used for spinal cord injury patients and persons having arthritis, cerebral palsy, Parkinson's disease, and back injuries. Offers professional education programs to instruct members of the medical and allied health professions in the most recent as well as most relevant rehabilitation practices and to teach rehabilitation personnel how to fulfill the special require-

ments of chronically ill and physically disabled people. (1942)
United Ostomy Association, 1111 Wilshire Boulevard, Los Angeles,
California 90017

Federation of local groups of persons who have lost the normal function of their bowel or bladder, necessitating colostomy, ileostomy, ileal conduit, or ureterostomy surgery, known as "ostomy." Aids in rehabilitation of these persons through material aid, moral support, or exchange of practical information in managing the stoma and its necessary prosthetic appliances. Works to educate the public as to the nature of ostomy with a view to ending job and insurance discrimination. Promotes and assists with research on management of ostomy and prosthetic equipment and appliances, and encourages study of the costs of rehabilitating ostomy patients. Publishes manuals and guides for ostomy patients, including *Ostomy Review*, a compilation of articles chosen from five years of *Ostomy Quarterly*. (1962)

NAME INDEX

177

SUBJECT INDEX

181